The Essence of Qigong

A Handbook of Qigong Theory and Practice

Ke Yun Lu

Translated from the original Chinese
by Lucy Liao

Abode of the Eternal Tao
Eugene, Oregon

Abode of the Eternal Tao
1991 Garfield St.
Eugene, OR 97405

Website: http://www.abodetao.com/

Cover photo: Huang Shan, China by Terry Caron.

Calligraphy by Wei Ping Lyn

Printed in the United States of America

ISBN 09649912-1-7

*Dedicated to Chen Hui Xian,
a loving and generous teacher
of qigong.*

Preface

Since 1988, I have written *Grand Master of Qigong*, *The New Age*, and *The Decoding of Human Metaphysical Phenomena*. In these three books, I have put forward a new thesis of study, namely, "human physio-cosmology." The synopsis of this new theory is as follows:

Its Formation

The theory has come into being during my researches and studies on qigong, human paranormal powers, and the various metaphysical phenomena in human life. To cite but a few examples: the myths of the *I Ching*, Jesus Christ, Sakyamuni Buddha, as well as the many occult techniques, esoteric traditions and myriad unsolved mysteries which have been termed "superstition" indiscriminately throughout the various stages of man's development.

In the cause of research on "human physio-cosmology,"many new avenues have opened up. Undeniably, superstitions abound. Nevertheless, to simply negate superstitions is itself another form of superstition, one based on the existing perceptions of our time and the many preconceived notions held by human beings. What we must do is not only negate yesterday's but also today's perceptions, and move forward.

In order to study these metaphysical phenomena, a supernormal method should be adopted. This is different from any conventional science. It requires that we synthesize all the results of the various domains and disciplines of human knowledge, combining Western scientific and analytical thinking with Eastern intuitive thinking, without which it would be next to impossible to have a perceptive understanding of human society nor access to "human physio-cosmology."

However, it is by no means one man's undertaking, be it research methodology or objective. It has to be a product of historical progression, coming into being at a certain point in time. Without the confluence of Eastern and Western civilizations, of modern and ancient cultures, such study would not be fruitful. Furthermore, without the large amount of preliminary research that has been made of qigong phenomena and human supernatural phenomena, and without the support of many ancient works, it is impossible for "human physio-cosmology" to come to its formation.

A Synthesis of "Human Physio-Cosmology"

From the macro standpoint, it is an anatomy of myths of mankind itself, a study of the mysteries of mind and body, soul and flesh, psychology and physiology, as well as mysteries of their interrelations. Much has been done in the study of human physiological and psychological structures. But understandably, more trails need to be blazed and puzzles solved.

"Human physio-cosmology" aims at studying and mapping out a new understanding of our universe. It proposes to study man's relation with the cosmos and with God. Hence, it is probable and possible to arrive at a new realization and comprehension of the meaning of spirit, material, the entire evolutionary process of the cosmos, and life itself.

"Human physio-cosmology" constitutes many other fields of interest. What is the relation between the *I Ching* and astrology? How do we understand Chinese Traditional Medicine and the meridians? What can be known about psychokinesis, telepathy and psychic healing? Can qigong possibly have any relation to psychosis, hypnosis, art, science, thinking, linguistics, etc.? All these need to be studied anew.

The Significance of "Human Physio-Cosmology"

My second book in the series on qigong has been titled *The New Age*. The third is a work on qigong theory, with *The Decoding of Human Metaphysical Phenomena* as its title, which I dedicated to "the twenty-first century." My own insight into the significance of "human physio-cosmology" should already be made obvious by this.

Contents

Foreword

We hear a lot about the ancient and mysterious art of qigong these days, everywhere from national talk shows to *Newsweek* magazine. Its adherents claim everything from stress reduction to a greater sense of peace, lowered blood pressure, better digestion, calmed emotions and even healing from serious health problems such as cancer.

While all these things are true and well documented in China, most people still do not understand how qigong actually works. Many qigong practitioners and even teachers do not really understand the many levels of qigong practice.

Most people in the West are introduced to qigong through a form or set of movements and visualizations taught by a specific teacher. They then assume that all qigong is taught and practiced in this way. The true essence or root of qigong is, or course, much more than doing forms or breathing exercises. It is an attitude toward life and our own energetic systems. It is an approach toward healthcare and personal lifestyle. It is a way to connect with the very deepest strata of being, down where we all have our origin, the very source of life, sometimes called Tao.

You will read of many amazing and seemingly unbelievable

feats and talents in this book. These things are possible for qigong practitioners because qigong works with the very life force that animates and dominates all life on this planet. By tapping into that powerful healing energy, qigong practitioners can do all sorts of amazing things such as remove pills from a sealed bottle, go without eating for months or even years at a time and cure themselves of many deadly diseases.

But qigong is more than just doing amazing feats and curing "incurable" diseases. Qigong is actually a deep spiritual practice. We work on our vital energy or qi (chee) so that we have the energy to support what is called the "emergence of the shen or spirit." In this way our true spiritual nature can shine forth and we can further ourselves not only energetically but spiritually.

The practice of qigong springs from the natural philosophy that is native to China called, in modern times, Taoism. Chinese medicine, taiji (tai chi), feng shui, energy meditation—all of these come from the vast well of Taoism. Nowadays there are many forms of qigong—Taoist, Buddhist and even Confucian, as described in this book.

But all types of qigong (and there are hundreds of styles in modern China) are based on nurturing, balancing and strengthening qi or vital energy. This qi has a physical aspect and a spiritual aspect. Qigong works on both of these levels, giving you two for the price of one!

The author, Ke Yun Lu, is very well known in China, where he has published many books. Before he began writing about qigong he published many books of fiction, describing the social conditions of his time. At one point one of his books was serialized on television and it is said that much of Beijing shut down for the hour his program aired because everyone was busy tuning in!

Ke Yun Lu has been researching qigong for many years and presents here the essence of this ancient yet completely up to date psycho/physical/ spiritual practice. By introducing the basic theories and guidelines to qigong, the author is able to provide a solid foundation for the Western practitioner, no matter which particular style he or she chooses to learn.

This book can be used by both the beginner and the long time student of qigong. There are too few experts on this subject in the West and because of this, the public is unable to differentiate between bona fide or false practices and teachers. By translating and publishing this basic handbook we hope to be able to offer guidance to students interested in learning more about how to find a teacher or style of practice that works for them and discovering what are the mysteries and pitfalls surrounding this unique and powerful practice.

Solala Towler
Abode of the Eternal Tao

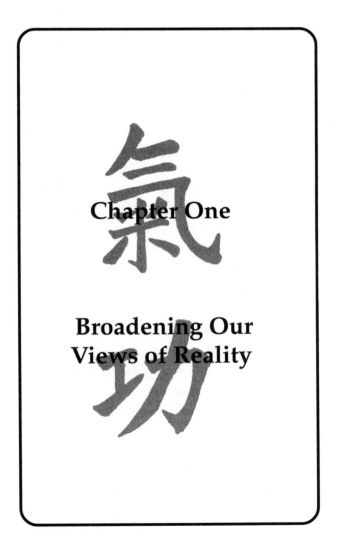

Chapter One

Broadening Our
Views of Reality

Every time I have an opportunity to talk with my readers, they ask me a host of questions. I am always tempted to say that if we observe from a new angle and level of thinking, the answers to most questions would not be all that difficult to find. For example, if you are walking on the streets of Beijing trying to figure out the grid without a map, all you can do is keep walking and walking. You may have to take many unnecessary twists and turns, and you will think the streets are a total mess. If, however, you stand at a vantage point above the city that commands a bird's-eye view, the layout of the streets would become clear. All the questions puzzling you would be answered. It is very important, therefore, to stand on higher ground, and alter one's thinking.

A year ago, I was given a chance to observe the performance of qigong master Shen Chang at a conference sponsored by the China Ministry of Broadcast, Film and Television. Hundreds of people were present for the event. A woman in her fifties entered the room. She had a tumor on her leg which was measured by the doctors to be about 7 centimeters in diameter. Under the watchful eyes of those present, Shen started qi transmission with a shout: "Gone!" Instantly the tumor shrank. Another "Gone!" further reduced the size of the tumor. The third time, the tumor disappeared completely; its disappearance was verified on the spot by the doctors. More astonishing yet, Shen could cause the tumor to grow back, and then disappear, again and again. He could also cause the tumor to grow in size. Finally the tumor vanished. The entire process was closely watched by hundreds of observers.

Another experiment of Shen's dealt with hair growth. Naturally, a number of bald men wanted to take part in the experiement. He picked a man with the baldest head possible. While dozens of viewers stood in a circle watching, he first shaved off what little hair was left on the man's head, then marked a circle with a ballpoint pen on the shaven part. Then he began to transmit qi, again with a shout, "Grow!" Everyone could see the pores beginning to bulge. With the second "Grow!" bits of hair began to show. Another shout and the man's hair grew about 1 centimeter long. After close scrutiny by those present, Shen used his qi to cause the hair to withdraw and then grow back. He repeated it three times.

These two simple instances were among the countless qigong phenomena I have personally observed. They were not magic tricks, nor were they a joke. The foremost guiding principle I set for my psychic research has been to eliminate the false and retain only the true. Any fraudulent show in the name of fake qigong and pseudo-science will find no place in my study. Only genuine cases are collected for the purpose of analysis. The above two examples may seem insignificant but they challenge the explanations of modern medicine and modern physics.

I have also made the acquaintance of a young woman named Ding who stopped eating since she attended a seminar given by the renowned qigong master Yan Xin in October 1987. Over the years, more than one research institution has monitored her health with various medical measurements. In the summer of 1990, a team of researchers conducted a round-the-clock observation of the young woman that lasted 30 days. With the exception of a small quantity of drinking water, Ding consumed no food of any kind. With the help of advanced equipment, the research team monitored her health in every way they could, including that of her digestive system, which showed no sign of food consumption. I met Ding again when she was an eighteen-year-old junior in high school. She appeared perfectly normal for a girl her age, and her grades were excellent. Five years earlier when she had stopped eating, her parents were worried sick. Before long, they were relieved to see that their daughter's health was in absolutely normal condition, and her school grades were getting better. She was growing both in weight and height. Her parents became convinced of the benefit of qigong. Ding's father is now an enthusiastic proponent of qigong.

Again, this is a true story. Under normal circumstances, a person who didn't eat for even ten days would be in grave condition, not to mention someone going for years without food. Ding has suffered no weakening effect, but has grown at the normal rate, both physically and intellectually. This is a miracle that cannot be explained by modern medical science. Similarly, it would seem impossible to remove a substance from a tightly enclosed bottle unless the seal is broken, but to someone with supernormal ability, such a feat is possible. When confronted with these phenomena, we realize the limits of science and our minds. We must realize that the world we live in cannot be explained by our past experience.

As we begin to probe qigong mysteries, human psychic powers, and human physiology and psychology, it is first necessary to change our pattern of thinking. If we limit ourselves to established patterns, we may be tempted to simply laugh away many important subject matters and easily lose the opportunity to upgrade human intelligence.

First, Attain Nothingness

Many of you may have heard this Zen story. A man went to a Zen master to ask about the secret of Zen. The master said nothing. He picked up a tea cup and started pouring tea into it. The cup was soon full to the brim, yet the Zen master kept pouring. The tea began to overflow. The man protested to the master, "The cup is full and tea is overflowing; please don't pour any more." The master then said, "That's right, when the cup is full it cannot hold more tea. When your mind is filled with other thoughts, how can you accept the Zen teaching you have asked me to give you?" This very simple story contains deep meaning.

More often than not, our minds are filled with numerous thoughts. Faced with something new, we usually construct a subjective framework out of our experience, theory, hypothesis, logic and knowledge. Such preconceived notions usually form the starting point from which we begin to study something, but they unfortunately also become the obstruction.

Your thinking, then, is far from free. Often when you try to tell a person about a phenomenon of paranormal nature, he or she asks many questions before you can even finish your explanation. That is because the moment the person hears it, his logical thinking machine begins to churn. To him, such things are too incomprehensible, too illogical, and too contrary to established theories. If you tried to answer every question he raised, you would be unable to because there would be no end to it. He would not understand, even if you tried every way possible to explain. It is advisable, then, to follow the ancient Zen master's method of a blow on the head and thunder: Change your way of thinking! Throw away your preoccupation with all your accumulated knowledge!

This method is easier said than done. It is more profound than it appears. Normally when a person is confronted with something new, he or she makes an intuitive judgment based on perception, logic, knowledge and theory. These reactions also intertwine with certain sentiments, impressions, and conflicts of interest. They tend to stiffen one's thinking. I call it hard-headedness. In qigong practice, they may prevent one from achieving higher levels; in Zen, it obstructs enlightenment; in thinking, it dims the spark of wisdom; in human development, it reduces the opportunity to invent, discover and create.

Surrender the Mind's Contents

In recent years, I have published volumes of work on qigong study. I have also interviewed many qigong masters and researched numerous psychic claims. More than once I have been asked by people impressed with my work how I have achieved so much in a relatively short time.

Let me tell you one secret: it is "nothingness," which means true humility, the kind that harbors no prejudice or preoccupation when facing something new. I have studied paranormal ability extensively, so that when I observe something new, I look at it without even thinking of what I already know. Even if it may appear to be quite ordinary, to me it is new. At such a time, all my previous experience, understanding, and all my work recedes into "nothingness." As a result, a seemingly insignificant event will very often trigger my inspiration and lead to new discoveries.

Nothingness: Maintaining a Relaxed State

Sometimes a person may be anxious to accomplish something. More often than not, anxiety may become so overpowering that it is difficult to let go. In such a state, how can one be free to think? For a qigong practitioner, where does qi come from? For you and me, whence health? whence inspiration? I am not advocating that everyone drop his or her duty, think nothing and do nothing. It is not so. The point is that we should maintain a relaxed state of being, eat our daily meals, sleep our nightly sleep and for some of us, write our novels and do our everyday work. What is important is to relax. You may say this is true enlightenment.

To Attain Emptiness

All too often we hear the terms "emptiness" and "nothingness" used interchangeably. Buddhism emphasizes the concept of emptiness. We will now look at it in terms of qigong practice.

Isn't it true that in the state of nothingness we let go our hard-headedness? That all our preconceptions, prejudices and restrictions are swept aside? Might we then say that the mind is being emptied into a blank?

In fact, no. Emptiness in this context does not mean a blank mind; it is a state of spiritual receptivity. A blank mind is just that, blank. It means nothing in qigong practice. If sitting and thinking nothing signified any advancement in practice, then a rock would be our best teacher. Such a notion is extremely misleading.

What is this state of spiritual receptivity? It means that when you are completely relaxed and empty of any desire, you will become receptive to inspiration. It is this spiritual illumination that forms the essence of qigong practice. It is also the source of our thinking, invention and creation.

There is one way to know it, and that is through experience. We can experience it in qigong practice, as well as in such daily activities as science, art and philosophy. This state of spiritual inspiration is very natural. One is so harmonious with life that everything becomes natural—be it working, sleeping or eating. In the words of Hui Neng, the sixth patriarch of Zen Buddhism, "Cease ye not a hundred thoughts," meaning it is a totally natural state. On the other hand, once you are in this state, whether you are tackling a problem of science or one of artistic creativity, you will find yourself full of inspiration and discovery.

Anyone can experience moments of inspiration at one point or another during one's lifetime. At such a moment, problems that surface can usually be handled quite naturally and without too much thinking. However, most of us rarely pay enough attention to it, and the spark of inspiration simply vanishes. Inspiration is not imaginary. When one is in a state of true inspiration, one can always make correct judgment. Throughout history, many great statesmen and military leaders, when faced with life or death decisions, would usually ask their aides to leave so they could be alone. Regardless of the numerous plans others may have drawn up for them, such leaders often pondered quietly before making a final decision. Why? They were waiting for that state of receptivity more often termed "inspiration" or "intuition." Some of the most critical decisions in history could not have been made without these inspirations or intuitions.

In the advanced stage of qigong practice, we call this"enlightenment." The presence of inspiration comes at that momentous point when heaven, earth and man are in perfect harmony. The secret of advanced qigong practice is to be able to reach that special point. When we practice, we should constantly try to stay in that state of inspiration, training ourselves to identify such a moment and grasp it. During years of research and writing, whether it is art, philosophy or qigong, I never wrack my brain. Even in the broad scope of research, with its many interdisciplinary subjects which sometimes seem extremely complicated and intimidating, I always try to stay in a state of emptiness and nothingness, letting intuition be my guide.

Some admirers call me a "diligent" writer, a term I don't particularly like. I would not think it accurate to call myself a hard working man. What is "diligence?" Considering that "you cannot become a Buddha without hard practice," diligence is all right. As a result of hard practice, you have reached the state of inspiration. Then, diligence would be something of the past, it would no longer play a major role. The value of your work is no longer measured by how much effort, but by how much inspiration. No amount of work would be commensurate with the inspiration of wisdom.

Ever since the publication of my works, many artists and calligraphers have shown more than fleeting interest in my research. Why is that? Because they also know through their own experience that hard work is a means to acquire the perfect skill, and once entering the state of inspiration, reliance on diligence is foolhardy. Isn't practice hard work? Indeed, some practitioners work extremely hard and, after years of practice, they reach a stage of tranquillity in which no disturbance can upset them any more. They are now in the state of inspiration, when hard work becomes less essential. No amount of hard work can lead one to the ultimate stage if no inspiration is achieved.

I am not a qigong master. Yet many qigong practitioners tell me they have been inspired by my works, and some of them feel themselves improved. How so? It is because inspirations are interrelated. My inspiration from the state of emptiness and nothingness is similar to that gained from qigong practice. To attain that state, one cannot rely on mastery over a rational mind, but rather on experiential knowledge of the heart in order to experience the emptiness that leads to spiritual receptivity. Pay special attention to that moment when inspiration descends. To grasp the right moment is indeed all that matters, be it in qigong, science, art, or in any other field of research.

To Attain Rootedness

One day a leopard forced his way into a herd of sheep and killed them all. When the young shepherd discovered the tragedy, he dashed toward the beast; shouting with fury, he killed the animal.

Imagine yourself to be the shepherd closing in on the beast, shouting with all your might. Feel for a moment how the energy in your body reacts. Next, suppose you are somebody watching from the side. You merely see the youngster rushing to the leopard. You may not experience the intensity, but you can still feel the fury, though to a lesser degree. Now let's say you simply watch the fight on television. You may empathize with the fury of the young boy, but it would be one step removed from the actual experience. If you only heard it from a recording, you may feel the youngster's rage somewhat but you would share none of his emotions. Finally, if all you knew about the story was an exclamation written on a scrap of paper, you would probably think it was some sort of greeting.

In the preceding example, we can see that the effect of the message decreased progressively from being the one who fought the leopard, to onlooker, to television image, to recording, and finally to the words written on paper. Each decrease causes the energy generated by the message to reduce manyfold. When in the end you only saw an exclamation written on paper, all that was left was some kind of notion, or concept. In Buddhism this is called "word mask." Without knowing the actual event, could you have understood what had happened when the exclamation was being uttered?

A lot of people like to read classics such as the *Tao Te Ching* or the *I Ching: The Book of Changes.* In the *I Ching* it is said that "one yin and one yang constitute the Tao." What can one get from these words? Someone may say it's easy to understand. Isn't it talking about yin and yang? We can't say this is an incorrect answer. However, when these words were being written in the *I Ching,* there had been more to the meaning; the words contained a lot of experience. Do you have that kind of experience? Without having such experiential knowledge, one's understanding can only derive from the words, from the surface. And that is what we call a "word mask." It is a far cry from the true meaning expounded in the *I Ching.*

I attended a seminar in Hohhot, Inner Mongolia, in the summer of 1992. I was asked to talk about Zen. To be honest, Zen is not something one can talk about, for anything that can be put into words would not be Zen. Of course, people still talk about Zen, and have for hundreds and thousands of years. So I tried my best to give the audience my own understanding .

I started by pouring myself a cup of tea and then spoke to

the audience: "You must all know what tea is. I just helped myself to some jasmine tea. Can anybody describe its taste?"

Many in the audience laughed. It was a simple enough question. One person said it had the flavor of a flower. The next one followed that it had the aroma of jasmine flower. Another one related that it had a bitter tinge. Someone else answered that jasmine tea has the flavor of jasmine tea, which was quite clever. And there were many more answers.

I then continued: There can be a lot more to say about what tea tastes like. First, try smelling it under your nose; can you describe the taste? Some might say it has a pleasant fragrance. Now, how does it taste when you have the first sip? What about another sip? The first cup, how does it taste? The second and the third cup? What taste does it have when a Southerner drinks it? How about a Northerner? What is the taste when one is happy? And when one is sad? How about when children drink it? Or elder folks? What if the tea is made with water from melted snow? Or from rain? When the drinker is enjoying tea leisurely? When the drinker gulps down the tea in thirst? So on and so forth; one can easily write an extensive book on "What is the taste of tea?" and give a thousand answers. Now let me put forth another thought: To someone who has never tasted tea, even when you can provide tens of thousands of answers and the most detailed description in the world, its taste will still remain some kind of abstract concept that bears no correspondence to what is really the taste of tea.

Which means, you cannot understand something that you do not know. Zen, or enlightenment, is difficult to put into language. Just as when we talk about telepathy, no explanation is enough if you have never experienced it. Why, then, do we still talk about Zen?

Let me again relate to the example of tea. Let's say a man had once tasted tea, but it was many years ago. His life has not

been easy, and he has had to toil to make ends meet. Years have
gone by, and the burdens of life have diminished his memory of
having had tea once before. He would not know what tea tasted
like any more. Yet you know he did taste tea in the past. Now you
start to tell him about tea, describing to him its color, taste, and the
different ways to make it. You are getting imaginative and tell him
that tea is like music, or spring water, or a painting, or even a poem.
You also talk about the sensation of tea being sipped into the mouth,
entering the gullet and moving down to the bowels, and so forth.
You keep on and on while he listens. Suddenly, one sentence in
your monologue triggers his memory and he lights up, murmur-
ing, "I remember." No more tea description and anatomy are necessary now. At that triggering point, he remembered the experience of tasting the tea. In other words, nothing can substitute for
your own experience—in this case, tea tasting— regardless of all
the advertisements and instruction manuals, theoretical syntheses
or artistic descriptions of tea.

Wisdom, which in Buddhist scriptures is called "Buddha
Nature," exists in every one of us. Because of the many restrictions
in our lives, however, it is clouded. We have lost our original nature. It is similar to a lamp which is dusty and dim from long neglect, and growing ever darker. All we have to do is scrub off the
dirt and dust for the lamp to shine brightly again. That is exactly
what "clear your heart and see your essential nature" means, because the light has always been bright.

Rootedness here means the origin of everything, of man and
of the universe. Zen teaching is like tea drinking. Every one of us
has tasted tea. If I want to remind you what tea tastes like, all I can
say about tea will be just words, the mask. It would be utterly unnecessary to you. The same is also true with Zen. If, out of numerous expositions, one hits home and awakens you to your true nature, then you can ignore all the rest. So the key is to seek out our

original root.

It is said in the *I Ching* that "one yin and one yang comprise the Tao." Yin and yang are the mystical starting point of Traditional Chinese Medicine. There is more that can be derived from these designations: life represents yang and death, yin; male represents yang and female, yin. Those having some knowledge about Chinese medicine know that spatial concepts such as outside and inside, exterior and interior, front and back, left and right denote respectively yang and yin. Relating to these concepts are far and near, high and low, south and north, east and west. Yang and yin also denote the notion of time, such as now and then, present and future. In terms of the properties, we have dry and moist, hot and cold, strong and weak, dense and loose, light and heavy, fast and slow, more and less, long and short, positive and negative, clear and vague. Denoting action, there are rise and fall, float and sink, expand and contract, forward and backward, attack and defend, give and take, increase and decrease, lengthen and shrink, add and subtract, multiply and divide, open and block. In our daily judgment we see good and bad, reward and punish, able and unable, beautiful and ugly, kind and evil, yes and no, love and hate, easy and difficult, which also correspond to yang and yin. Why is there such consensus of yin and yang, that heat should be yang and cold, yin? This is the so-called "The One gives birth to the Two," which is the origin of the "root." This designation reflects the primal essence of the universe, and mankind has conceptualized it through the division of yin and yang.

Nevertheless, we have not grasped the essence if we only remain on the conceptualization of yin and yang. Quite a few people have studied the *I Ching* their whole lives but have no clue as to its true meaning, simply because they devote all their attention to the conceptualization of yin and yang.

When you are called to distinguish the yin and yang of a

matter, such as above and below, or masculine and feminine, normally you have to stop and think. What results from thinking has to be logic, whereas true understanding of these divisions has nothing to do with logic or the mind, but is a kind of experiential feeling beyond words. For instance, the designation that the back of our body is yang while the stomach is yin cannot be a theoretical formula or logical deduction. Such distinction only reflects the original state of the life form. We may say that the *I Ching*, Traditional Chinese Medicine, or acupuncture have not developed a summation of logic but rather are the result of intuitive formation of which no language or logic could claim any part.

This rootnedness, therefore, requires that we break out of the language trap of all preconceptions and ideas to reach the origin of all things. Return to the Origin, and all the Ways lead back to the One. The root of the Origin is the "Tao," it is "Simplicity."

To Attain Openness

In China, we usually associate the notion of openness with that of the circulation of blood and the meridian connections. Sometimes when problems emerge we will also say that our thoughts are open to solutions. It is indeed a descriptive term to use. When one's thinking is open, the body usually responds accordingly. In the same vein, if one's thinking is not open, certain organs in the body may also be blocked. It may seem strange, yet our mind and body are truly connected and related in such a close nature. To take it a step further: we need to interrelate such disciplines of study as psychology, physiology, physics, linguistics, anthropology and cosmology, as well as human thinking. There are many human thinking patterns, such as emotional, imaginative, aesthetic, intuitive, and also psychic, subconscious, and dreaming.

Likewise we can expand our thinking by connecting Eastern and Western cultures, combining the most rational and logical with the most intuitive, so we do not adhere rigidly to one or the other. Openness plays a crucial role in handling problems. Trying to be open helps a lot. Many of us who have studied foreign languages may all go through such an experience. When you want to translate some broadcast from the radio, you cannot linger too long on any particular word. The radio may go on and on, and you may be stuck with one word you do not know; you cannot concentrate on its meaning for too long or you will miss the rest of the content. One correct way is to follow the whole piece without paying too much attention to any particular word. It is all right to miss this or that word, just get an idea. That way you will not miss more. Such is the knack in learning a foreign tongue. The same idea can also be applied to the learning of qigong, or even to one's own life. One cannot be rigid in the search for truth. Stay open to all aspects. It is important to integrate different disciplines and achieve a thorough understanding of their interrelationship.

Chapter Two

The Theory of Qigong

The recent increase of interest in qigong throughout China is a phenomenon that has not been seen in many decades. Yet qigong is not something new. It is a time-honored legacy from the longstanding civilization of the Orient.

The earliest available record of qigong was written about four or five thousand years ago. As early as that time, perhaps even earlier, our ancestors had already gained excellent mastery over the art and technique of qigong. When society did not include crowded skyscrapers and highly developed technology, man enjoyed a very intimate relationship with nature. Our ancestors lived, on the one hand, a very harsh life because of limited means. On the other hand, their consciousness of self, of both body and spirit, was much deeper and sounder than modern man's is today.

Qigong developed from man's intimate connection with nature. Renewed interest in and research of qigong cannot be said, however, to represent man's closeness to nature, but on the contrary, his distance from it. The popularity of qigong inevitably indicates man's desire to get back into harmony with nature in a time when modern life is so full of contradictions and confusions and he can find no balance.

In daily life we are often forced into a state of tension due to different factors, both personal and social. We must constantly masquerade and twist ourselves. You may not agree with me and retort "Whence all the tension and disguise?" In response let me ask you, are you as casual at home or by yourself as you are on other occasions? Surely you need to show some manners when you are in the company of others. In a way, this can be compared to an elastic rubber band. It hangs naturally. When you twist it for a long stretch of time, its shape becomes distorted. However, once you stop twisting, after a while it will bounce back to its former shape.

Any prolonged twist and suppression of oneself can only result in disease. Man is destined not to be able to remain in his natural state and act as he wishes. What is the way out? One alternative is to relax and release the tension from time to time, so as to straighten the twist and readjust our body and mind. There are many ways to readjust and relax. Qigong is one that is both easy and effective.

Some time ago, I read about a person who came across some sketches in an archaeological study. After careful textual analysis, he was convinced that those sketches were illustrated instructions for a form of qigong. He started practicing by imitating the movements in the illustrations. Soon something strange happened: his wife would fall asleep every time he did his movements. Before long, he developed a very strong hypnotic power and has since given many public demonstrations. It did not matter whether you believed he could do it or not. Regardless how hard you tried to resist, you would be hypnotized in a matter of minutes as soon as he started his movements. He never failed.

The Validity of Qigong

Qigong has been around for a long time. Its power is beyond any doubt. At first glance, confidence in the benefit of qigong may seem simple and elementary. This is exactly where the effectiveness of qigong lies. One's belief in the validity of psychic and paranormal powers very often becomes conducive to the acquisition of such power.

In China, many people know about Zhang Baosheng, who is adept at paranormal feats. Somebody once asked Zhang, "How do you remove pills from a seamless bottle?" Zhang answered, "You can do it, too." The questioner was puzzled. "How can that be possible?" he asked. Zhang replied, "First of all you have to believe in yourself, and second, just tell yourself in your heart that "I must get those pills out of the bottle!" Third, scratch the bottom with your fingers." All said and done, most of the people would not be able, after all, to attain such tour de force even if they followed Zhang's coaching to the letter. Why is this so? It is a question of the fineness of true belief, which comes not from rational judgment but from a conviction in the heart.

I know a person with strong healing power. He has cured many of the rich and famous. He is especially adroit at curing breast cancer. All he has to do is make a gesture of grabbing at where the tumor is and it vanishes then and there. He has cured thousands of female patients, among whom there was no lack of medical doctors. He told me, "I can take away the cancerous tumor in another's body. But I just cannot take something out of a sealed bottle, or a cigarette from its box." (Understandably, what he meant was to "take out" something using mental power.) He then asked me what the matter was. I mentioned my theory to him and he agreed. "Yes, I am always convinced that I can take away the tumor from one's body, but I have a hard time convincing myself that I can mentally cause a cigarette to be removed from the box. It just would not work, whether I try talking myself into believing it or forcing some kind of confidence in myself."

Belief and disbelief are at the same time the most elementary and ultimate factors in qigong. Here lie all the secrets of qigong practice. The recent popularty of qigong has made public numerous case studies. Many believers have been won, yet more remain skeptical. A lot of people dare not believe what they have witnessed. The reason is deep-set, because the qigong phenomena run against our rational and logical knowledge, which become obstructions to our understanding.

Previously I talked about the four elements that are instrumental to enhancing one's qigong attainment. The first one is "nothingness," which means we need to overcome any preconceived notions or ideas. "Nothingness" represents a state of mind, though not a blank mind. You may practice Buddhist or Taoist qigong. You may do movements or meditation. Regardless of which school you follow, you must first of all cast aside all your desires or preconceptions, and naturally bring forth a faith in the benefit of qigong. That is the secret of effectual practice that can help a practitioner advance to a higher level of attainment, even within one day. It will be quite ineffectual to just talk about qigong technique without such instinctive understanding.

Many books and magazines on qigong have been published containing numerous cases and examples. Try to analyze them, discarding the false and misleading information. Look at those facts with objectivity and select one or two cases you believe to be true and convincing; try to experience it and come to your own understanding. A momentous flash may awaken you to a higher level of understanding, of self-awareness. It is indeed possible if you believe in the true nature of qigong.

The Meaning of Qigong

In a sense, qigong is a convenient term. It can be explained as the process of relaxing ourselves into a natural and tranquil state, when our body and mind undergo a natural readjustment and regain their original harmony with the universe. At any rate, this is the best summary of qigong we can give in modern language.

As to the various schools of qigong in China, there are Buddhist, Taoist, Confucianist, as well as medical qigong, martial art qigong, and many folk qigong practices. If we are to give qigong a more limited definition, then it can be said that any form of qigong provides a complete set of methods and techniques for the nurturing of our body and spirit.

On a macro level, the definition of qigong extends far beyond methodology and technique or its general benefit on our body
and mind. Neither is it a simplistic generalization of metaphysics.
It is a complete system of practice, encompassing issues of world
view, our moral and ethical systems, as well as practical matters
such as body and mind improvement. Qigong really should be
understood in a broad sense, and that is the perspective we will
explore in this book.

Qigong and the *I Ching*

The *I Ching: The Book of Changes* was a classical work of the
Confucian culture, having historically been revered as the first book
of all classics in China. I have stated in one of my recent books, *The*
Decoding of Human Metaphysical Phenomena, that the *I Ching* had
taken its inspiration from qigong, which is the element most fundamental to its coming into being.

The *I Ching* is composed of two parts, "The Book of Oracles"
and "The Book of Biography." The former, "The Book of Oracles,"
was largely based on the experience obtained from divination by
generations of oracles. Generally, such practice itself was conducted
in a near-state of qigong. When ancient men performed divination, an elaborate ritual of fasting, abstaining from drinking, kill-
ing, or any disquieting behaviors would be followed by a cleans-
ing bath before the event. Then incense would be burnt, and the
diviner would enter a peaceful trance, beseeching assistance from
the spirits. He would enter a state of qigong. It is then reasonable
to say that all the mysteries and secrets of the *I Ching* come from
qigong.

In the course of time, many sages and philosophers, including Confucius, gave the book numerous interpretations and com-
mentaries and, gradually, the *I Ching* evolved to be the most significant work of the Confucian culture. It truly became a book of

wisdom, with its concise and profound aphorisms, axioms, and comments giving reflections on things as far as the cosmos, or as close as daily existence. As the book itself becomes firmly established as a complex embodiment in civilized history, people are inclined to forget its original reason and state of being. For some time, its oracular use has been accused of being ridiculous and nonsensical.

In the *I Ching*, the most significant underlying principle is yin and yang, about which we have gone into length in the previous chapter. The understanding of yin and yang and their polarization comes from non-logical thinking and an interruption of logical reasoning, which is beyond all verbal formulations. If someone tries to identify, through theory only, that above is yang and below is yin, exterior yang and interior yin, masculine yang and feminine yin, he is a long way from comprehending the *I Ching*. True comprehension should come spontaneously, and without needing reflection. Once you achieve such an experience, you will grasp everything. Once you fathom qigong, you will comprehend the *I Ching*, and you will understand all.

Qigong and the Buddhist Scriptures

First of all, notice that Buddhist qigong is different from Buddhism, which should again be differentiated from Buddhist philosophy. As a religion, Buddhism has a long history. Its study, which embodies sociology, philosophy, history, culture, psychology, physiology and folklore, is beyond the scope of this book. Briefly, from the viewpoint of qigong, many Buddhist scriptures reflect an understanding of qigong on very advanced levels and comprise some liberal views on the universe, as well as the relation of mind and body. My intent is not to encourage or endorse any particular religious belief, because that is an individual choice.

I simply want to point out that, in both the past and present, man has found common ground in practices of uplifting the mind/body, regardless of locations, races or religious beliefs. As a human being of modern times, one should not be biased toward any one of those, whether it is for the benefit of the individual or for the development of human civilization. They all merit our attention and objective study. Therein lies the value of Buddhist scriptures.

Qigong and the *Tao Te Ching*

The *Tao Te Ching* is the classical work of Taoist qigong. It has exerted great influence on Chinese culture for over two thousand years. Taoism, together with Buddhism and Confucianism, comprise the three origins of the Chinese cultural tradition.

The *Tao Te Ching* is composed of only five thousand Chinese characters, yet in them can be found political and military strategies as well as the wisdom of life and living. It has been the subject of numerous debates and discussions. I do not intend to make any sociological or philosophical critique on the *Tao Te Ching*, nor to evaluate Lao Tzu, its author, and his personal views of society, for without doubt he had his individual preferences. Honestly speaking, I do not worship Lao Tzu, because we need not worship any sage, but face him equally. Only in this way can we achieve an objective understanding of something or someone.

Neither worship nor disregard is helpful. The habit of positioning someone higher or lower than yourself is really an unnatural way of making distinctions. Try to treat something or somebody in a natural and undisturbed way.

What makes the five thousand words of Lao Tzu such an embodiment of wisdom, and so widely applicable in areas so vastly different from one another? First of all, the Way of Heaven and the Way of Man are invariably connected. In the *Tao Te Ching*, Lao Tzu related his experience obtained from his extraordinary state of consciousness. At the same time he interwove his understanding of life with society, history, and philosophy, with heaven, earth and man. In the works of Lao Tzu, nature and society, society and man, are organically connected. That is the wisdom of Lao Tzu. We can leave the other judgments to the rest of the world. Similarly, a qigong master of the highest attainment may have a somewhat unusual taste for food, and when he makes comments on certain food, you need not be overly critical, for his preference is his alone. Otherwise we may be trapped in the pitfall of seeing the tree only. The point is to discern the subtlety of the *I Ching*.

Also, the *Tao Te Ching* delineated a comprehensive system for qigong practice, everything from world view to technique. We must effect an understanding of the original meaning of the *Tao Te Ching* beyond the superficiality of its words, for, "The Tao that can be spoken of is not the constant Tao."

Qigong and the Bible

In the Bible, one is bound to read about the miracles performed by Jesus Christ which, in modern terminology, were his supernatural healing powers. For example, a faithful woman was cured of metrorrhagia; a bed-ridden fellow was made to walk; a deaf man was given hearing; and a neurotic was made normal. Another fact one may notice was Jesus' ability to teach and convince. How did Jesus conquer the world? Really, all through the two thousand years, it is his supernatural power and his persuasion that have made the world listen.

Some people give Jesus' miracles a highly mysterious aura, insisting on their being the act of God. On the other hand, there are people who totally dismiss the Biblical miracles as false or legendary, which adds little to our understanding. In fact, all these become not only explainable, but also understandable if they are put into the perspective of qigong and the phenomenon of human psychic power. Let's say this powerful master was also an exceptional teacher, imparting social and moral teachings that fit in with people's needs at the time. Under such circumstances, it would not be incomprehensible that a large group of followers gathered and thus a religion formed.

With observation uninhibited by conventional perceptions, you may discover that Jesus was in a very special spiritual state, lasting not only days, but months and years. His miracles performed on the sick, his extraordinary power—aren't they the same as we have time and again observed in our qigong research today?

When facing any historic event, we should maintain a natural stance, neither overbearing nor compliant. The further evolution of civilization necessitates a reassessment and re-evaluation of the significance of all human metaphysical phenomena, including religions. Man can only realize himself through his renewed understanding of Jesus Christ, the Buddha, Lao Tzu, the *I Ching*, and the various mysteries attached to them.

I will continue to voice my opinion in the course of my research, so long as I can see and experience and understand. My conscience is clear when I bring forth my own conclusion regarding these important issues, not being intimidated by consensus or authority. "When the Tao rules, even spirits retreat." This is also a state of qigong: aboveboard and straightforward, completely at ease with oneself and having nothing to fear.

Qigong and Traditional Chinese Medicine

I have always maintained that in our Chinese culture, as far as works of qigong are concerned, there are three classics; i.e., the *I Ching*, the *Tao Te Ching*, and the *Huangdi Nei Jing*, *the Inner Classic of Medicine*. The *Huangdi Nei Jing* is a medical classic written in the second century BCE. It is also a classical work about qigong.

As a matter of fact, the fundamental mystery of the entire work is qigong. Only when we understand the *Nei Jing* from the perspective of qigong can we begin to unravel its esoteric meaning. Of course, it wouldn't be strange that many traditional Chinese medical practitioners and theorists disagree with my viewpoint. Part of my work from now on will be a series of studies on the exposition and theorization of my argument. Traditional Chinese medicine would lose its most fundamental validity without the inclusion of qigong, which is repeatedly referred to in this ancient medical manual.

If we can get a thorough grasp of the principles of yin and yang through qigong, we should then not only be able to understand the depth of Traditional Chinese Medicine, but also develop its theoretical system. According to traditional Chinese medicinal theory, not only drugs, but all foods are characterized by their properties. So is it true with the whole existence of nature. Society has its properties, as well, though this is not included in the *Nei Jing*.

One may observe the varying effects of a certain type of social life upon one's body and spirit. Surely being in a natural environment or in a bar will not only cause your mind to react differently, but also cause different bodily reactions. When our mind-body equilibrium is upset, we can rebalance it through the use of medicine or food, or through the readjustment of our social life. Its mastery, of course, is beyond such a simplified synthesis. To sum up, everything in our universe is interconnected and interrelated.

Qigong and Wu Shu
(the Martial Arts)

Wu Shu is directly associated with the principles of qigong. Among its various forms, people are most familiar with tai chi (taiji), such as tai chi chuan (taijiquan) and tai chi sword movements. The essence of tai chi is not its movements, though they are important. It describes mind awareness, qi (chi). There lies its essential secret. Tai chi is wholly based on the art and principles of qigong. The primitive and unformulated movements, from which modern tai chi chuan originated, must have sprung from spontaneous motions induced by the qigong state. These movements have been developed by generations of practitioners, eventually evolving into their present forms, with the purpose of conducting energy movement of the body using simple, formulated movements.

When we talk about "mind" and "qi" in taijiquan, many people know that mind leads the movement of qi, which follows the direction of the mind. My personal understanding of qigong leads me to believe that the foundation of tai chi is mind following qi, the mind feeling the flow of qi. In this process, qi circulates naturally, while the mind follows without deliberate effort. In contrast, if mind is to lead the movement of qi, what happens if the qi fails to follow? That is the secret of tai chi, as well as that of the Taoist qigong, and any forms of advanced qigong practice.

One may ask why many martial art instructions, especially those focusing on attacking movements, all emphasize that it is the mind leading the force and the qi. The answer is because that is more from the application point of view, it is more pragmatic. Nevertheless, the "original rule" of mind and body, the practicing of mind-body wholeness, undoubtedly calls for the mind to experience the flow of qi.

Buddha and Maya, Tao and Demons, Spirits and Witchcraft

I have been asked by many readers whether spirit and witchcraft are the same, and what differentiates them. I tell them they are both qigong phenomena, but of different natures; they are the varied visions arisen from qigong practice; and they are the different moral behavior of qigong practice.

The way of Buddha, Tao and spirit is actually a qigong reality, or a higher reality, which has had a positive influence in history. In a similar way, the realm of Maya, demons and witchcraft also belongs to such a reality, which since antiquity has found varied expressions in many remote and primitive regions, and has been frowned upon by mainstream qigong schools. An example of this is the sorcerer's exorcism dance in the Chinese villages of old times. On such an occasion, a person would suddenly be seized by some kind of unknown power and fall into a trance state. Then some happenings unbeknownst to the person are foretold. This is a primitive form of psychic prediction, which may have certain functions, such as healing or forecasting. But it may be harmful, too. It is superstitious to give it total credulity and is just as superstitious to discard it as simple superstition. They belong to certain supernatural phenomena (or what we call the qigong state), are unknown to man and should be studied with equal effort.

The way of the Buddha, Tao and spirit, and the realm of Maya, demons and witchcraft are also two sets of expressions describing the two effects, or levels, of qigong. The first signifies the positive effects, or the higher levels, while the latter denotes the negative effects (such as the so-called Maya state, or overbalance), or the lower levels. In qigong practice, when one achieves the state of "nothingness" and "emptiness," inspiration sparks and enlightenment dawns. On the contrary, qigong practice may also bring forth visions or illusions. One may see all kinds of demons, spirits, enchanting beauties or palaces. Again, this is the realm of Maya and it is imperative that we are able to discern them in our practice.

The way of the Buddha, Tao and spirit, and the realm of Maya, demons and witchcraft symbolize the hierarchical levels in qigong practice, with the former belonging to higher or more advanced levels, and the latter to lower or more elementary levels. Many ancient legends record the struggles between these levels: Buddha and Maya, gods and demons. In the end of the battle, the Buddha was triumphant and the gods victorious while Maya was defeated and demons were conquered. In this duel of the sacred and the profane, supernatural power is the weapon, whether for the divine or the devil. However, the underlying distinction is their relative levels, or power. In reality, our qigong practice also contains different levels, and it is incumbent upon us to seek the levels of the Buddha or the Tao instead of that of the Maya or the demon.

The way of the Buddha, Tao and spirit, and the realm of Maya, demon and witchcraft further summarize the morality of qigong. The former embodies the goodness of mankind while the latter represents harm to mankind. At the various levels of qigong there are varying moral standards of behavior. If qigong is used as a means of engaging in lawlessness and perpetrating outrages, it is usually defined as the realm of demon. On the other hand, when qigong becomes an instrument for promoting societal wellness, assisting the needy and healing the sick, it is the way of the Buddha. We certainly must follow the way of the Buddha in our qigong practice.

Qigong and Shamanism

For most Chinese people today, shamanism is a very derogatory term. Throughout Chinese history, Confucianists as well as Buddhists and Taoists have viewed it as some sort of wicked and demonic practice. In reality, however, when supernatural power is involved, the way of the Buddha and Tao and shamanism are interrelated and differ only in their levels of power.

First of all, paranormal or psychic power underlies the core of shamanism, which is one of the oldest cultural traditions of all peoples and nationalities. There are two kinds of intrinsic power in man, one being the natural and the other supernatural. In primitive societies, when man was still in his infancy, paranormal phenomena were much more common. Shamanism has been defined as "an arcane art employing fabricated unnatural power for the purpose of realizing a certain wish." In fact, this power is neither "fabricated" nor "unnatural." It is a mystical power that is imbued deep in our physical as well as psychic bodies. Man cannot comprehend it, although he has worshiped it. This supernatural power or shamanistic practice is practically as ancient as mankind itself.

From the very beginning of mankind's existence, we have been confronted with three forces: one, the force of nature, the irresistible forces of heaven and earth, of the sun and moon; two, the intrinsic force of man himself, knowable, comprehensible and controllable; and three, the mystical force of human supernatural power. These three forces were often regarded as one, which is understandable considering the unfathomable, unpredictable and mystical forces of nature. To our ancient ancestors, the worship of natural and supernatural forces was one and could not be separated.

Shamanism worships mystical power, which may belong to natural or to human supernatural forces. It makes no differentiation and combines the two into one force, with the resulting deification of nature. Such worship forms the origin of all primitive religions and, indeed, that of the various religious beliefs in latter times.

On the other hand, shamanism has its wisdom and is able to forecast changes of nature, and heal, which eventually evolved into such scientific disciplines as astronomy, medicine and meteorology.

We can be fairly sure that the concept of shamanism came into being before shamans. In ancient tribes, supernormal power must have been possessed by more than one person, since for many of the ancient beings, the power was naturally endowed. Nonetheless, differences in degree existed and may well have resulted in a "division of labor" and gradually become concentrated in a certain person. Specialized shamans came later as a natural process. In antiquity, shamanism played an especially significant role in human activities; as a result, persons who had mastered the shamanistic art, we can imagine, held enormous authority over their people.

Shamanistic functions were often full of various rituals of mysterious authority. Such rituals served as a means of hypnosis or self-hypnosis, which was essential in bringing into play the paranormal power in the shaman, or in shamanistic healing ritual, adjusting the response of the healed. Some of these practices have been absorbed and utilized by religions that emerged later.

As human history evolves, the role and status of shamans and shamanism diminished. Gradually, to the majority of people, shamanism has become a mere means of making a living with some esoteric performance.

There are three factors to such a shift of perception. First, as modern science and technology develops and productivity increases, man has become more and more the worshiper of scientific achievements. Second, religions such as Buddhism, Taoism, and Christianity have matured and undergone tremendous development. Third, the secular government has become less and less dependent on shamanism in its rules.

From the beginning, shamanism had manifested both the wisdom and ignorance of mankind. Its inability to explain supernatural power and the worship of such power showed its ignorance. And as shamanism became diminished, its ignorance may sometimes be reduced to chicanery. Yet, it is without doubt that paranormal phenomena have always played a role in shamanism.

Qigong and Paranormal Power

The existence of human paranormal or psychic power has been proven true by many replicable studies. In the recent decade, Chinese researchers of many scientific disciplines have done a large number of convincing experiments. In my book, *The Decoding of Human Metaphysical Phenomena*, I classified the types of human paranormal phenomena into about twenty categories. Nowadays, there are many stories about supernatural incidents. I wrote extensively about Wang Youcheng from Jilin Province of China, a man with very interesting psychic abilities. Wang is a close friend of mine. In 1990, I made a careful investigation into his paranormal claims. He told me that his ability was induced at the very moment when, in 1976, a gigantic meteorite fell from the sky in Jilin. Since then, his life has been closely linked with this meteorite. As a staff member of the Jilin Museum, he is directly in charge of preserving the fallen meteorite and all the pieces from the main heavenly body that can be recovered. His many uncanny powers are beyond the scope of this book, but here is just one minor example.

One of Wang's abilities is to stick coins to his forehead. He can stack more than twenty coins at one time to his forehead, as long as he is in good mood. In between each coin, a sheet of paper can be inserted and pulled back and forth. On one of his bad days he was able to stick as many as six coins on his forehead with much ease. Those coins I pulled out from my own wallet on the spot, and no tricks could possibly have been made on them. After he did it on himself, he turned to me and started to stick coins on my forehead ! A sheet of paper was layered between each coin, and a total of six coins were readily stuck on my forehead. When somebody pulled the paper, those around me could even see the coins whirling on the paper.

Afterward I asked him how he had come by this ability. He told me that once he made a visit to a Buddhist temple and saw a golden triangle between the eyebrows of the Buddha's statue. He thought that was very strange and all the way back from the temple he could not stop contemplating it. Suddenly he realized it was a sign of paranormal power. As soon as he got home he experimented on his own forehead and soon realized he had developed this extraordinary feat.

The above example is meant to show that people with psychic abilities may need to go through an "opening up" process. The correct attitude toward paranormal power or psychic power is an extremely sensitive issue because it somehow puts our conventional knowledge to shame. It may also attract skepticism, opposition and criticism from antagonists because it is antithetical to our conventional knowledge and experience.

Modern physics claims that it is inconceivable to remove pills from a tightly sealed bottle without breaking it. Yet in reality, a psychic can do just that. He can transport the solidly sealed pills from the bottle, with all eyes centered on him. How could physics explain this anomaly? Scientists may have to face the uneasy issue of paradigm shifting. The theories and beliefs of the physicist or medical specialist are incapable of explaining such a simple act and this failure is threatening to their status as "expert." It is necessary that they refute their theories but they are unwilling to take such a leap because, after all, those theories have made them the authority in their field. Such an issue is undoubtedly a very sensitive one. At present, every discipline is invariably confronted with the issue of how to keep its position tenable. If all the paranormal phenomena are true, science will have to be rewritten. At such a point, what is superstition becomes a penetrating issue.

There is an authoritative international organization called "The Committee for the Scientific Investigation of Paranormal Claims." Among its members are celebrated scientists, distinguished scholars, and famed magicians. It also has two Nobel Laureates. According to the Committee, so far none of the so-called psychical claims are true.

A few years ago, the organization sent its investigators to China for a special study. It announced that if only one incident could be proven successful and true through vigorous scrutiny, they would highly award the performer with prizes. Unfortunately, nobody came forth to give any demonstrations and the investigators left China, even more convinced that there is no such thing as paranormal phenomena.

In my other books I made a solemn appeal, challenging them to make another investigative tour through China. I am willing to assist them in searching for persons with credible reputations who will give convincing demonstrations. Man's prejudice can truly hinder his ablility to obtain the truth.

Paranormal Power
In Your Qigong Practice

The term "paranormal power" is interchangeable with "supernormal" or "psychic" abilities. In qigong practice, oftentimes practitioners will induce, as a result of practice, paranormal ability of some sort. This may include clairvoyance, telepathic diagnosis, extrasensory healing, prediction, telekinesis, and many more. How can we understand these paranormal abilities?

One attitude held by some practitioners is that all paranormal powers are a result of advanced practice. Some practitioners, because of this belief, are so eager to attain these supernormal abilities that not only do they not achieve them, but they may develop certain syndromes of mental disturbance instead.

Therefore, it is important that qigong practitioners refrain from mere pursuit of supernormal abilities. If you feel physically and mentally healthier or more relaxed in life because of your qigong practice, or you are more efficient in work, more cosmic in outlook, more innovative in science and creative in art, then you are in very good shape. It is really unnecessary to develop psychic power.

If you do acquire some psychic ability however, do not feel nervous, frightened, or ecstatic. A rule of thumb is to refuse nothing and miss nothing. We do not need to block the development of any psychic ability, because it is nothing sinister, but it is bound to happen at certain stages of practice. Sometimes when we continue our practice, the psychic powers disappear. Just let it take its own course. Some practitioners are very stiff necked. A few of them, impatient to open their Tianmu (the brow chakra, or third eye), have gone so far as to poke their Tianmu point (between the two eyebrows) with a twig and consequently have injured themselves. What purpose does this serve? Such attachment is painful. In qigong practice, extreme behavior such as this often causes a negative reaction of qi.

Qigong practice calls for relaxation, naturalness and tranquillity before one can enter the state of qi, which is self-awareness and well being. When you stubbornly pursue something, you are not tranquil or relaxed. How can you achieve the desired state? The occurrence of paranormal ability very often is the upshot of unintentional success from intentional practice. You are practicing serenely, with no particular desire in mind. Then suddenly some phenomenon occurs and it becomes a kind of supernormal power. It is what we call unintentional fulfillment. Never should we have such unfounded belief in psychic powers, nor should we cling to its pursuit. Just allow it to take its natural course.

From the standpoint of qigong practice, paranormal powers belong to the realm of arcane art, which is not the highest achievement of the Way or Tao. To achieve enlightenment and to attain Tao should be the ultimate pursuit of any qigong practitioner.

Some people tend to disregard and even disparage the phenomenon of psychic ability. Many times I have met practitioners or masters of qigong who vehemently dismiss paranormal power as absurd, low-level psychomancy. This is again incorrect. For qigong practitioners, paranormal power is a phenomenon that is bound to occur at certain stages of the qigong practice and, generally speaking, it is a reflection of one's advancement as well as one's attainment of higher levels. It should be congratulated, not slighted or dismissed. In fact, paranormal powers can be employed to heal disease. As long as one maintains an objective perspective on these supernormal phenomena, and does not engage in dangerous pursuit of such powers for some selfish purpose, they should be regarded as a milestone on the path toward enlightenment and wisdom, which are the highest levels of qigong practice.

Possessing paranormal power and occult skills does not necessarily guarantee that the practitioner has attained the wisdom and enlightenment which characterize the higher levels of qigong practice. I have come across quite a few people with paranormal abilities who seem to be at the very low end of qigong attainment. They are confused about the world and their own life. Some of them are actually neurotics and have lost control of their mental awareness. Obviously, this is not a form of high level practice. Conversely, anyone who has realized enlightenment and attained wisdom is sure to possess supernatural power. This is what the saying "magic power comes from your nature" means.

On the other hand, by willfully playing down the function of paranormal power, certain self-professed "enlightened beings" unwittingly reveal their lack of such abilities.

A practical position on supernatural ability should be one that is objective, with no superstitious pursuits nor unfounded belittlement. It ought to be known that the occurrence of paranormal power signifies a positive effect of qigong practice, which marks a certain degree of attainment. It should also be known that the occurrence of paranormal power comes naturally and cannot be sought for, nor can it be forced to happen. Refuse not when it comes and pursue not when it passes.

The Scientific Attitude

The following, in my opinion, describes the scientific attitude toward qigong:

First, we should maintain that paranormal phenomena exist and accept them as the unsolved mysteries of our human society. Seek truth from facts. Every fact should be established according to scientific investigation.

Second, we must realize that, from ancient times to our modern world, many unsolved mysteries have shown intricate links to human paranormal power and qigong.

Consequently, if we can solve the puzzle of human paranormal phenomena, we may hold the key to all mysteries ever existing throughout history. The outcome of this research will modernize all the scientific disciplines of mankind.

Qigong, Suggestibility and Hypnosis

Those who do not believe in the efficacy of qigong, including scientists who are suspicious of qigong, often tend to give it a simplistic definition. Vice versa, many qigong practitioners and enthusiasts repudiate such a view and disclaim any association of qigong with suggestibility or hypnosis.

The truth is, this question is so complex in and of itself that it could be the subject of more than one book. Concisely, the relationship between qigong and suggestibility and hypnosis can be followed in this way: It is obviously true that, to a large extent, qigong practice employs some techniques of suggestion and hypnosis, which form an integral part of many qigong activities and phenomena. It does not in any sense degrade qigong by such an association, but shows the interrelatedness of all human wisdom.

An experiment was once made in which someone who claimed to be a qigong master gave a "seminar" to transmit qi. As soon as he stepped onto the podium, many in the audience started to make involuntary movements. He then told the audience that he was not a qigong master and they were moving because the suggestion he had given worked. It is not strange that such a thing can happen, which also explains the significant effect of suggestibility. There is no need to deny the use of certain suggestion and hypnosis techniques.

Therefore, whether qigong employs suggestibility or self-suggestibility, hypnosis or self-hypnosis, these ways appear to be effective for preparing one for entering the qigong state. It will be very beneficial if, in the course of studying qigong, we also investigate the various effects and benefits of suggestion and hypnosis.

I have discovered in my studies that suggestion and hypnosis have been used in religious experiences since ancient times. Only by acknowledging this fact can qigong study maintain its objectivity.

As we argue that qigong activities involve some element of suggestion and hypnosis, we must also emphasize the fact that qigong in reality involves certain elements that entirely evade explanations by suggestion and hypnosis.

Several years ago a television documentary about the famed qigong master, Yan Xin, was produced for China Central Television. At the time they started the documentary, the director bluntly stated that he did not believe at all in qigong. When they were ready to film Yan healing a bone fracture using qigong, the director himself went directly to a hospital and selected one patient with a serious comminuted fracture. The doctors made a complete check, recording and photographing every detail, and finally put the patient in a cast. Everything was done to the minutest detail. The next day, Yan Xin came to the hospital, with the camera closely following every move he made. He started talking with the patient. After several minutes, Yan told the patient to remove the cast. The fracture had already been healed completely. X-ray showed no sign of the bone having been broken at all. The patient could move his arm, which had been put into a cast only the day before, with total ease. This was just one of the numerous incidents that were filmed. By the time the documentary concluded, the director had become an enthusiastic advocate of qigong. I do not yet know of any such healings resulting from suggestion or hypnosis therapies.

There is a type of paranormal power called telekinesis. I have observed too many examples of telekinetic incidents to recount them one by one. Briefly, to remove pills from a tightly sealed bottle or to break or weld metal needles by will power, and so forth are examples which have all undergone strict scrutiny by scientific researchers and can be verified by records, investigations, and studies. Of these, even the simplest experiment could not be accomplished by suggestion or hypnosis.

Suffice it to say that, on certain levels or to certain degrees, suggestibility and hypnosis share certain similarities in technique with qigong. Nevertheless, the effectiveness of qigong goes far beyond the limit of suggestibility and hypnosis.

Qigong and Psychiatry

In qigong practice we sometimes come across the problem of practitioners being influenced by "evil spirits." Someone with an unstable mental condition may be induced, in the process, into some form of mental illness. Such incidents are rare, but it nonetheless happens. In our qigong study, it is important to accept such incidents, however infrequently they may occur.

These incidents occur because one, the most basic requirement for practicing qigong is to relax, which means that we relieve
ourselves from the control of our reasoning, preoccupation and
logical thinking process. We simply think of nothing. The second
reason is that by relaxing our rational thinking, our subconscious
is brought to the foreground. Or we call forth the power of both
the Buddha and the Maya, or God and Satan, at the same time.

The inner, unconscious power cannot be brought into play
unless we loosen the grip of our rational thinking. It is impossible,
however, to awaken only the positive side of the unconscious without its negative counterpart. It is then imperative that we master
the most important skill, which is to eliminate negative influence
and attain spiritual inspiration, enlightenment, or Buddha nature.
Sakyamuni Buddha encountered many Mayan illusions and dis-
turbances on his path to enlightenment. That is what we call "the
Maya influence."

Why does the Maya influence occur? In modern terminology, our suppressed desires, wishes and fears are released in the
course of practice. It is similar to the human dreaming process: as
soon as we relax, dreams appear. Oftentimes our dreams are of a
most ridiculous nature. In the course of our practice, visions and
illusions may appear and it is important that we know their nature. We must pass this stage and rid ourselves of their disturbance
so as to realize the true enlightenment that comes from the natural
inspiration of heaven and earth harmony.

A few of those with mental instability lack positive
willpower and, as a result, may be disarrayed by the Maya or negative forces. This not only manifests in qigong practice, but also in
the form of various obsessions in daily life, which may very well
become an inducement of mental illness.

The structure of man's consciousness is a complicated system. If we can combine qigong phenomena with psychiatry in the study of the human subconscious and explore the deep structure of human consciousness, many truths can be revealed.

What should we do when negative force interferes? The answer is simple. Regardless of any visions, be they pleasant or frightful, try not to indulge in such a state. Keep our "true heart" calm and tranquil, set our mind on the higher levels of practice. Most of us have the ability to surpass this stage. In the case of the few in want of will power, the careful guidance of a powerful master of high attainment can help to safely pass it. The very few with a history of unstable mental condition and without the guidance of a master will risk the danger of mental disturbance, once rational control is lost. Therefore, as a general rule, do not suggest qigong to such a person.

Qigong and Modern Medicine

It is not unreasonable to say that the supernatural power attained through qigong practice has gradually materialized in the form of medical technologies. Man's psychic clairvoyance and telergy are being manifested in wide applications in modern medicine, such as X-ray or sonography, as well as various other tests and measurements. No doubt these modern technologies all correspond to man's preternatural abilities. It shows that all modern technologies are in reality a form of extension and externalization of human potentials.

Because modern technology is a manifestation of human potential or human supernatural powers, we can say that qigong has its positive effects and is beneficial to mankind. However, we should never think that qigong can replace medical science. I am a big fan of qigong, but I must say qigong has its purpose, as does medical science. We should be able to see that most of man's ailments are cured by medicine, and it would be erroneous to discount the effectiveness of medicine simply because we practice qigong.

On the other hand, although qigong cannot replace medical technologies, it can do something that modern medical science cannot. For instance, psychic healing can cure cases in which conventional medicine has failed. That is one of the advantages of qigong.

Qigong also plays a unique role in maintaining mind-body health as well as preventing diseases. Further studies of qigong and a better understanding of its fundamentals will result in still more effective medical technologies.

Besides its potency in healing and rehabilitation, qigong can be most efficacious for inducing physical wellness and psychological balance. We practice qigong not for the sole purpose of healing and strengthening our body, but also for something more profound. An author may experience more inspiration after practicing, and the same can be said for a scientist. No medicine can give us spiritual inspirations. Fancy some kind of injection called inspiration. There is no such thing! But qigong can bring us into a spiritual world, which is the most wonderful part of our practice.

I want to ask those who believe nothing about qigong to please not categorically deny its function and the relation of modern medicine with human supernormal abilities. Do not think that modern medical technology can be developed without studying human psychic powers. Let's pay special attention to this ancient, yet new phenomenon. Conversely, to those friends who are so enthusiastic about qigong as to be biased against modern medicine, I want to say please be highly alert to such one-sidedness because it can also be a grave mistake. It is very important that we put qigong and modern medicine in the correct perspective, establishing a relationship of mutual information sharing and promotion.

Qigong and Its Relation to Zen

Nowadays it is fashionable to talk about Zen—Zen this and Zen that. Books on Zen are hot sellers all over the world. But a lot of these are mere "verbal Zen," played on lips.

Many qigong schools share a close relationship with Zen, including Chan Mi (Intensive Zen), Chan Yi (Zen Mind), and Yi Zhi Chan (Single Finger) schools.

What is the relationship of qigong and Zen? First we must realize that, in general analysis, qigong and Zen are not the same. Second, they are nonetheless connected in terms of inner realizations. Third, if we are to look at qigong from a macro point of view, then a high level qigong state is in a sense a state of Zen. Fourth, the similarity of the two, since we confirm they are in essence the same, lies in what we have discussed in the previous sections; that is, enlightenment, Buddha nature, or our true self.

The Present State of Qigong in China

Many people have asked me to write about the present state of qigong. I must say that in China today, qigong has undergone a natural evolution. More and more people are beginning to accept the rationality of qigong, and it is certain to see further development. Its irrational aspect will inevitably be subject to the control and adjustment of our social organism. Let us be frank and natural. Have no baseless optimism or unfounded pessimism about its progress; there is no need for impatience. Do not expect any dramatic highs, but do not lose faith. A good thing will naturally grow, just as our discussions come naturally.

At the same time it experiences growth, qigong will also encounter hindrance and opposition, which is not at all strange.

Qigong is gaining more and more attention in the world, and there will come a day when the whole world looks at qigong and studies its revelations and problems from the vantage point of science and philosophy. Then, qigong will play a more important role in our society. We have good reason to believe that this wish will come true.

Chapter Three

Qigong Mysteries
and Practices

Who Can Practice Qigong?

In theory, anybody can practice qigong. There are many styles of qigong, and different people can benefit from different routines. However, to the few who suffer from mental illness, or have unstable mental conditions, one restriction must apply in spite of the theoretical presumption that everyone is fit to practice: they must be under the close guidance of an experienced and adept qigong master. Because it is difficult to guarantee such guidance, they are generally advised not to engage in qigong practice. Other types of physical training would be more suitable. With the exception of the above, all others—male and female, old and young— are fit to practice qigong. Naturally, a qigong style that best suits your individual condition would be the most beneficial both to your mental as well as physical state and even to your life.

Transmitting Qigong From Ancient Times

People who are curious about qigong may wonder how qigong masters impart their knowledge and how students learn the routine. They soon find that most students begin their practice by following a certain instructor and a particular routine. They may then begin to wonder just how many teaching methods have been used throughout the history of qigong. Based on my research of numerous historical qigong records as well as through my own practical experience, I have concluded that the following five methods are used:

First is the method of guiding demonstration, which is the one used by most qigong masters and instructors. In accordance with the progress of the student's skills, the master or instructor gives a step by step demonstration of the practice routines, and at the same time explains and expounds some qigong theories.

Formula, the second method, is a step higher than the first one. Formulae often relate to some restricted higher degree practice.

In the third method, the master gives no demonstrative instructions but only talks, either in a few words or in effusive speech, depending on his or her individual style, about the morals of practice. The entire Zen practice, as well as Buddhist qigong and even the methodology used by the founder of Buddhism, Sakyamuni Buddha, all have this in common.

The fourth method is transmitting, or bestowing power. The Guan Ding (sudden realization) method of Buddhist qigong belongs to this category, in which the master transmits, through power of mind, his inner power to the disciple, who immediately experiences immense improvement in practice.

The fifth method is the communion of heart to heart, or initiation. This is widely used in Zen practice, and combines the third and fourth methods into a comprehensive and more advanced procedure.

Many qigong masters or instructors adopt one or the other of these five methods. It helps to know this, because you then know when and how to receive the messages conveyed by the master.

Seeking a Master

Following are ways one may go about seeking a qigong master:

One, a student may seek only one master in a lifetime.

Two, a student may have more than one master. To be more

accurate, he or she may seek different masters at different stages of practice, or seek several masters during the same stage of practice.

Three, a student may experience self-cultivation; that is, receive no instructions from any teacher. This usually happens as a result of natural and special circumstances such as during a thunderstorm, earthquake, or meteorite falling, when one's potential psychic power is suddenly awakened. Very often, powers induced in such a manner can be strong and intense, but the person may lack proper understanding of such qigong phenomena, and may have difficulty staying in control. Such a person can easily go astray and remain on the lower level of self-realization.

Four, a student may not study with any particular instructor, but instead draw experience from everyone. He or she learns from all things that are useful and meaningful, and teaches himself or herself the essentials of qigong.

Generally speaking, the four methods are not absolutely separate but are often interrelated. Regardless of which method one adopts, one common rule is to respect the master. We should respect anyone or anything that has been of assistance to us.

By respect, we do not mean the enslaving worship of the master. In qigong practice, modesty and simplicity always help a person receive energies from different sources. Someone without much education may follow a master sincerely and humbly, and learn very quickly and make great progress. His neighbor may be well-educated and very intelligent, but somewhat dubious of qigong or qigong masters. It is true he also learns qigong, but does so condescendingly and will get nowhere.

We certainly need not idealize qigong, but to disregard it won't help us understand it either. It is important to be humble and to pay our respects to qigong, to our masters, and to anyone who has done us favors. This is also a good way to practice.

Choosing a Practice and a Master

Many people ask me which qigong style or form they should learn, and want to know which master they should follow. Almost all practitioners are certain to wonder what path they should take, whether they are at the initial stage of practice or are advancing to a higher level. The answers to these questions vary according to the many masters and different schools of qigong. Nonetheless, all truths are one. I shall go beyond the details of each school of practice to focus on the ubiquitous nature and the general rules of qigong practice, which can be proven true by any test.

The foremost principle is to "accept the natural occurrence." Let me show you an example of what I mean by this. You may follow the School of Fragrance or you may practice the Soaring Crane style. It is all right if you follow the School of Silent Wisdom. It is also all right to learn the Kongjin gong or the Zen qigong. What practice you choose is most likely to have resulted from opportunities of one kind or another that happen to come along at some point in your life, having much to do with your socio-economic status, individual experiences and social circles. For instance, a seminar on a certain practice of qigong may have been given in your area, and you happened to be there. You had the time and desire to learn, and there you started. Or when you were visiting a friend, you chanced to meet a qigong master whom you really believed and trusted. You were eager to follow the master and the master was also willing to instruct you. Soon you were on your way. So when you start training naturally with a qigong form because of some disposition of fate and circumstance, that is what is destined for you. Whence the meaning "to accept the natural occurrence." Choices made in this way are rarely misguided.

However, sometimes you may have to face making a deliberate choice as to what routine you are to learn, and your friends have also made available many masters whom you can follow. It is very difficult to decide which is the best to choose. Under such circumstances we can apply the following three principles:

First, there are many names of many different qigong practices and upon hearing them, you like a particular one the most.

Second, you have met a number of qigong masters but somehow only one inspires your total trust even the first time you meet.

Third, you may have tried a few qigong routines before, but as soon as you start practicing this very one you feel completely at ease.

If these are the cases, then you can be sure of which qigong you will practice and which master you will follow.

We have discussed the two aspects of which qigong practice to follow and which master to seek: to accept the natural occurrence and to follow the one you like most, trust most and feel most at ease with. Having understood the intricacies of these secrets, you will have no difficulty in following your judgment despite the disputes and varied opinions others may offer. The three intuitive decisions you readily come to may very well be the judgment of your intrinsic nature. That is true knowing. We ought to honor this insight because it embodies many of the mysteries of qigong.

Learning Other Practices

If a person has already been practicing one style of qigong, is it practical to learn another style and is it advisable to do so?

This question has a quick answer. When you fully comprehend the mystery of qigong, the right way comes easily. If you want to learn another practice and yet are hesitant and indecisive, then it's best to consult your heart—if you are definitely determined and solidly prepared to go ahead with the new practice, and you feel no reluctance in giving up the previous practicing routines, then by all means do it. When a practitioner is advancing in his or her practice, chances of having to make such a decision are inevitable. Most high-level qigong masters typically have studied and practiced under more than one master. They roam about the world and seek worthy masters. It is highly improbable that a responsive practitioner who is intelligent and alert would follow just one practice all his or her life. When you feel that you want to learn another form of qigong, try not to dwell on too much doubt or concern in your mind.

For quite a number of practitioners, however, it is necessary and advisable to concentrate on one particular practice within a certain period of time. It is said that "single-minded practice is more beneficial than many a diversion."

Time and Place of Practice

When to practice? Different qigong schools have different requirements. In general, any time of day should be fit for practice; otherwise, the ideal of being in a qigong state twenty-four hours a day would not make much sense. That is a non-formulated way of practice, however. Usually when we talk about practice, we talk about rules.

We live and function in society, and most of us have different lifestyles and work schedules. So, what is the best time to practice?

The first thing to consider is convenience. It is important to know what time is suitable for you because all too often it is the inconvenience of time that discourages the practitioner from carrying through.

The second consideration is finding a quiet time with the least disturbance. It can be early in the morning or late at night.

The third consideration is somewhat subtle. It has to do with the particular moment of heaven-earth harmony. According to many experienced practitioners, from 11:00 pm to 1:00 am—near midnight—or around the noonhour are usually the best times. What is the rationale behind this? One may point out that it is quiet at midnight, but it is more than just that. During midnight practice it is more important to feel the shifting of yin and yang energy. Midnight is the deepest part of the night, when the element of yin is at its peak. However, the element of yang is also on the rise, when deep night gives way to the coming of a new dawn. A process of change is taking place. Usually we talk about the harmony of heaven, earth and man, and that is part of this mysterious cycle. When we do midnight training, the main thing is to be aware of the alternating force. So it is not only the quiet moment we are looking for since we can find quiet at other times.

Pertinent to the place we choose for practice are the following three principles: convenience, a quiet place without disturbance, and the delicate temporal relationship.

Qigong practice requires a certain place or environment. Theoretically, any place will be fine; even when you are in Wangfujing, the most crowded part of Beijing, you can still do your routines. Quietude is a comparative concept. If you live in the city it would not be realistic to retreat to the deep mountains just to practice. However, try your best to secure as noiseless a place for practice as possible. In addition, it is important that you are conscious of some connection to the surroundings, which somehow makes you very responsive.

We have discussed some guidelines for choosing the time and place for practice. Now, in terms of actual qigong routine practice, what do we need to know? Following are the ten tenets of qigong practice.

Tenet One: Tranquillity

Lao Tzu said in the *Tao Te Ching:* "Take emptiness to the limit; maintain tranquillity in the center." In other words, immerse oneself in a state of tranquillity. It is the basic of basics that one be able to keep a peaceful mind. To be able to remain in a state of deep tranquillity is a prerequisite to attaining higher qigong state, and is the core of practice.

The first consideration is whether we can achieve that state of tranquillity. Practically every practitioner has come across this or that difficulty, or had this experience or that attainment. For beginners, it is always difficult to relax and quiet down. This may not be a problem for someone who has a more receptive mind and whose body naturally relaxes when the mind quiets down. But for most beginners, it is very difficult to quiet one's thoughts and re-lax the body. They usually need to relax their bodies before their minds can calm down.

Then, how can we enter this tranquil state? Handed down from a long time ago is a qigong saying: "substitute ten thousand thoughts with one." It is so basic that to practice any qigong forms or routines, particularly in the elementary and intermediate stages, no one can expect to go anywhere if it is not first achieved.

What exactly is "substituting ten thousand thoughts with one"? How do we do it? Following are some answers.

First is to adjust the body. This applies to the general medi-tation routines, including standing and sitting meditation. While either standing or sitting, try to loosen up your body—muscle, blood circulation, bones and countenance. When each and every organ in your body is relaxed, your mind will naturally follow. This method is easy to do and is efficacious to many. Someone who has never done qigong training should first ease off the fore-head, then the eyes, and feel the effect; next loosen up the whole body, from head to heel, inside out, and untighten the muscles until there is nothing between the bones and the muscles. Little by little, the mind also quiets down.

Second is to control one's breathing. There are quite a few

breathing exercises and many books are available about methods that can be used. You can adopt any kind of breathing method as long as it helps you relax and is also convenient for you. Although there are various levels of breathing control, general practitioners should only be concerned with convenience.

Third, focus attention on certain body parts; for example, concentrate on the *dantien* point. This point of concentration replaces all others and gradually one enters tranquillity.

Fourth, try chanting mantras. This is essential for the Buddhist Pure Land qigong, which teaches no other methods other than chanting the mantra, "Nammo Amida Buddha." You can do it in silence, or in a low voice. After chanting this mantra day in and day out, you will do it without any conscious effort, even without uttering the sound. You can walk on the street or do other things, yet the rhythm of the mantra has become so instilled in your consciousness that the sound, audible or not, produces its effect. There is no mystery in Buddhist mantras or other incantations; they simply substitute endless thoughts with the singleness of mantra recitation.

For example, say you are talking to an old country woman. It would be quite irrelevant if you try to teach her all about qigong theory. All you need to do is tell her to chant "Nammo Amida Buddha," and after chanting thousands and thousands of times she will have the blessings of both spiritual wellness and physical health. Chances are she will be so immersed in the mantra that all other thoughts are dispelled and she will have achieved the desired tranquillity. She has no more worries and her health is regained. As a result, her family benefits and that is a blessing.

Fifth, concentrate on the routine. Different schools of qigong teach different routines, which are sets of body movements, together with regulated circulation of qi, the energy, and point of attention. Some schools stress the importance of the mind. Others claim that mind plays no part in their practice.

Right now in China, Fragrance Qigong is very popular. Many practitioners of this style claim that it is good to practice Fragrance routine because it involves no mind. It is simple and effective. Normally I make no comments on the alleged pros and cons of various styles of qigong. Yet in this case, when one does such routines as Phoenix Nodding, Dragon Tail, or Bodhidharma Rowing, one certainly gets some idea of the meaning of such titles. What is in your mind when such phrases flash by? That is a thought—a good one, though. Also, it seems to be pure movement without thought when you are doing the routines. Nonetheless, the act of doing movements contains thought, a single-pointed thought that dispels all others. This is yet another example of "substituting ten thousand thoughts with one."

I must be honest and say that all the popular forms of qigong are not high level ones. Advanced qigong routines are generally transmitted in encoded forms by the masters. Regardless, even these popular forms and routines simply will be of no use if they ignore the function of the mind.

I will give another example to make my point. Kong Jing qigong also emphasizes pure movements. It equates its routines with the circulation system of the human body; for example, the movement of each finger corresponds to a specific blood vessel. Its movements can cause strong energy flow in the body. Again, it claims that mind has nothing to do with the movements. But even so, one needs to concentrate on the motions to be able to practice well, which is not different from concentrating on the meridian points. All in all, these simple routines are easy to follow and offer a good start for beginning students.

For every qigong form, especially on the elementary and intermediate levels, the most fundamental issue is to be able to enter deep relaxation and direct your mind to a single point of attention instead of being swamped with myriad thoughts. I hope to open a clearer way of looking at the different forms and moves of qigong, and to facilitate your practice. Such understanding will also help you gradually and naturally find the way that fits your individual needs. Better yet, you may be able to come up with ways that can help you relax faster.

A lot of qigong movements have interesting names, such as those we mentioned earlier and others like Holding the Sun and Moon, Embracing the Universe, Standing on Snow Mountain, and so forth. They all connote some positive message, which infuses the practitioner with a certain psychological association. Imagining traveling through the infinite light of the universe or imagining being totally transparent can certainly help with one's understanding of the movements. Therefore we can see the purpose of these titles. Would you like a movement that is named A Mouse Crossing the Street? I think not.

The next thing to do is desist thinking, which means in the process of quieting down, cease any thought the moment it emerges, instead of letting it run wild. Usually the mind will pop up with new ones, and it is important to halt each one as soon as it arises. Before long, you will acquire the ability to shut out any unwanted thoughts, and eventually you will be able to do it without ever being conscious of the process. This is the high level you should seek. Again, it is to "substitute ten thousand thoughts with a single one." The single thought is used as a means to halt the ten thousand thoughts.

The last step is to "conquer without conquering." You can read about this in the Buddhist Diamond Sutra. What does it mean? Say you are agitated, and your mind just will not calm down. What can you do? Just ignore it. Yield to it. Make no effort to subdue it. In the long run, the mind will surrender itself, and thus you have conquered your mind without conquering. This is also of a higher nature, which is more difficult to attain.

When you try to quiet down, your mind is unlikely to cooperate readily. It churns out all kinds of thoughts. At such a moment, you need to sit quietly, trying to figure out where your "true self" hides. Through the eye of your true self, try to observe your mind. It may run in every direction, but your true self can manage it. In due course, you will enter a state of deep meditation despite the resistance of your surface mind. The deep tranquillity and the surface flow of thoughts can co-exist. However, your original mind remains undisturbed even when thought seems to be still flowing on the surface. This state of mind is of a much higher level.

The Sixth Patriarch of Zen Buddhism, Hui Neng, once said, "I myself possess no talent, but I never cease thinking." What he meant was that amidst the turmoil of mind activities, his true mind remains peacefully undisturbed. Just like the ocean in the storm—underneath the surges, it remains calm and serene.

We have discussed the seven ways of achieving tranquillity. Once you are able to make them thoroughly your own, all the mysteries of qigong will become clear.

Why is it that calligraphy can help you enter tranquillity? Before starting to use the brush, you wash your hands, dust the desk and lay down the paper. In the old times, people also lit incense. You then sit straight and hold your brush. Now you concentrate on one thing only—doing your calligraphy well. That's it! The numerous thoughts are now replaced by only this single one, and you easily enter the state of qi.

Tenet Two: Experiencing

By experiencing, we mean that when you are practicing qigong, try not to involve any intellectual analysis. Forget all that you have learned and known. Of course, when you are not doing the routines, you should learn as much as possible about qigong theory. Think about it. Talk about it yourself. Listen to others talk about it. Turn it over in your mind. Try to understand it. But when you are doing the routines, think of nothing. No theory. Instead, experience every movement.

This perspective may not be shared by some practitioners. That is all right. Even so, try not to think too much. Just keep it in mind. Sooner or later you will experience its meaning. If not, keep on and it will sink in. It is most important to experience with your heart and with your soul.

Tenet Three: Nothingness

In qigong practice, "nothingness" cannot be overstressed. We need to set aside all our attachments to levels and achievements, even to qigong itself. "Nothingness" is really a transcendental state, a natural state of being.

For instance, a group of people gathers together. Somebody in charge tells them not to stand too close, so they quickly disperse. Now the person in charge asks them to please stand more naturally, and everybody begins to assume a more natural posture. They probably did not realize that the way they stood before making the adjustment was the most natural, since nobody was conscious of it. As soon as they were reminded to "be natural," the spontaneity was lost.

The moment of spontaneous posing can be referred to as "nothingness," the most natural state of being. It is also analogous to our qigong practice. You do not have to be too fastidious about each move. Just try to relax. Flow through it.

Tenet Four: Emptiness

I have gone into great length on this topic in the previous section so I won't repeat myself.

While we maintain an empty state of mind, our bodies undergo certain changes. They are involuntary. I will not go into detail since that may create certain visions, which may become a hindrance in our practice and lead us astray.

Just pay attention to the changes that take place in the state of pure emptiness, that moment of divine inspiration.

Tenet Five: Rootedness

No matter what school of qigong we follow, it is essential that we experience its origin. The same is true with looking at our world: go beyond the surface, the image, and the perception until you get to its origin.

A book is produced with paper. The paper is made of trees, straw or other materials. The trees and straw are grown in nature. Nature forms part of our universe. And where does the universe come from? On and on we reflect on the original state of our world. In the qigong state, we can often experience miraculous phenomena.

Tenet Six: Openness

Let me first show you an experiment that can be done during meditation. As soon as you calm down, try to imagine that you can see the meridian points in your body. Some of you may be able to actually look inward and see the channels. When the images of these points appear, imagine again that all the points in your body are open and connected. If you keep on visualizing, your body will experience certain changes. You then imagine that not only your body organs are linked, but your mind and body are connected, too. Through this experiment, you may experience the wonder of qigong.

My research tells me that whenever our minds are blocked, our bodies will be affected by the blockage as well. When you are caught in a difficult situation, you may pull a long face. Don't think it is just your face showing the anxiety; your entire body also is burdened. If you ease off your facial muscles, your look will be relaxed and your body will in turn loosen up. Life is a material form of interrelations. Your facial expression is connected with your body organs.

It is known in modern medicine that through a single hair we can know the health of a person. Similarly, in Traditional Chinese Medicine, the ear-acupuncture therapy, with needles applied to one's ears, can cure ailments in other body organs, for example.

When your brows are knitted because of worry, not only is your body knitted, but your internal organs are also tightened into knots. We often use such phrases as "my heart was in my mouth," "it makes my blood curdle," "it delights the cockles of my heart," and so forth. These are not just descriptive terms. They relate to certain body and mental states. When a person is fearful, his face shows it. His heart also feels the dread. On the other hand, when a person is serene, not only his facial expression tells it but his body feels the peace as well. We need to observe and understand our body-mind relations.

In my work, *The Decoding of Human Metaphysical Phenomena*, I wrote that "our facial expression is our transient and changeable physiognomy which is in turn our permanent and fixed facial expression."

A person may be born with a good-looking face, but if he or she has been overburdened by the hardships of life, then gradually the look becomes one of distress. A sad face does not look nice. Sometimes the genes may carry it to the next generation.

When you feel mentally distressed, your digestive system may also suffer. Stomach disease, indigestion, and distress are all related. Long term depression may lead to heart ailments. This is now common medical knowledge.

Pay special attention to keeping a peaceful mind. When practicing, signal yourself to open up, to connect every artery and channel of your body.

Tenet Seven: Oneness

To be one with the universe is the ultimate state of qigong.

Many qigong guidelines tell us to merge ourselves with heaven and earth, be in harmony with man and universe, and embrace the cosmos. These are some basic principles of qigong practice. However, at higher levels of practice things may be different.

These guidelines are a good way to initiate practitioners into qigong. On the other hand, their overemphasis can be paradoxical. It may become a subjective desire rather than the actual experience, which can lead to illusions. It is important that we reach a state of pure harmony with the universe through our own practice and experience. Do not rely on what the masters say or what the books say. We need to experience this by ourselves.

Tenet Eight: Compassion

To be compassionate and loving means that we should be kind to everything and everyone. Those who have a kind heart can be close to the state of qigong even without practicing. On the contrary, a person who always harbors unkind thoughts may find it extremely hard to do well even with incessant practice.

From a macro viewpoint, compassion and love form the psychological mainstay in our daily lives as we practice qigong. Of course, for a compassionate and loving person, there will be unavoidable moments of trouble, suffering, anger, or narrow-mindedness. It is perfectly understandable and we should not be overcritical.

Say for example a person gave some much needed assistance to an old man who is in a life-threatening situation; the giver would feel very happy and in a good state of mind. If he did his qigong routines at such a time, the effect would be very good, too. He may have a marvelous experience. On the contrary, if a person was engaged in something shady and then did his routines, a negative effect could result.

To be compassionate and loving enables us to better receive energy from the universe. Vicious thoughts make us out of sorts with our environment, hence attracting negative energy. Being compassionate and loving is not only a psychological requirement but also a basic practicing skill.

Tenet Nine: Harmony

The concept of harmony should be understood in the context of qigong. It does not mean that we should not fight against the evils in our daily life.

To maintain harmony is more than what etiquette requires in our speech and in how we deal with people. More importantly, we need it in our qigong practice. Maintaining harmony all around us is in itself a state of being. In Chinese language, harmony contains the meaning "soothing the qi." Cultivate harmony with yourself and the universe. When you are in harmony with heaven, the earth and all beings, you harmonize the various life forces into yourself. Try to experience it, feel it and understand it.

While in a group, an adept qigong practitioner can immediately sense from its energy field whether the group is in accord. When we detect disharmony, then we do our best to bring back the harmony, to synchronize the energy flow. It is a way to practice and improve oneself. If a practitioner diffuses discord everywhere, he causes pain. He is then far away from his goal of maintaining harmony.

Tenet Ten: The Way

Again in the *Tao Te Ching* it says, "Man models himself on

the Earth; The Earth models itself on Heaven; Heaven models itself on the Way; And the Way models itself on that which is so on its own." This means man should observe the ordinance of heaven and earth, while heaven and earth operate on the laws of the cosmos, and the cosmos complies with the principles of the Tao. Ultimately, the Tao follows the prescript of nature.

Following nature is the ultimate achievement of qigong. Model ourselves on that which is so on its own. Accept and take whatever is natural.

Visions in the State of Qi

I have become acquainted with many qigong practitioners. Quite a few of them have seen visions in the course of their practice. These visions are of all kinds of things. Some see demonic creatures; others see strange animals. A few see scenes of paradise, or the image of the Bodhisattva of Mercy. Some see their departed friends, others see their relatives who live in a distant land. Everyone seems to see different things. Many practitioners are confused by these visions and do not know what to make of this phenomenon.

If you see visions, first try to distinguish real ones from false ones. Many qigong masters speak about the message being true or false. What is a true message? Let's say when practicing you induced certain psychic powers. You saw the vision of a friend being seriously ill. A few days later you received a letter that confirmed your telepathic message. That is then a true message. You should be positive about it.

However, we must realize that most of the visions that appear in the qigong state are illusory and produced by our subconscious desires. Sometimes what you dread most will appear in your vision and what you desire most will also appear in your vision to tempt you. If you are eager to attain high levels, Quanyin

Bodhisattva may appear in your vision. There are some people who claim to be the reincarnation of the Supreme Jade Emperor, or the master of the Buddha. Such fantasies are often born out of one's unconscious megalomania.

We must make a distinction between the real and the false. Try to be positive about the true messages, examine them and experience them. It is a way to develop your potential powers. At the same time, count out all the false messages and eliminate them with determination. This is also necessary and essential for our practice so that we may stay on the right track.

Secondly, we can disregard and dismiss any visions that appear, whether good or bad, beautiful or vicious. Simply ignore them. Just think of it as part of the process. This attitude is the best for every qigong practitioner. For those who aspire to achieve the highest level, this is the only correct way.

Some qigong disciplines and their practitioners are too fascinated with visions that appear during their practice. They see Quanyin Bodhisattva, or the Buddha, or the God of Universe, or Emperor Pangu, the legendary creator of heaven and earth in Chinese mythology. I have tried to advise and caution these people that they should dismiss and ignore whatever visions they may see and just maintain the peace of the original mind. I remind them of the saying, "Maya or Buddha, get rid of them the moment you see them." Keep in mind that all this is illusion, and it is best to cut them off with the mental sword of wisdom. A true believer of Buddha would understand. A high level of practice opens up wisdom and brings enlightenment and the discovery of one's true nature. At this advanced stage, see everything as illusory, be it true or false messages. The only thing of importance is to maintain the true self, one's original mind. This is the path to wisdom and enlightenment, to the ultimate state of qigong.

Of course, in certain stages of our practice, in order to develop our potential, we may use the first method discussed earlier, which is to distinguish true messages from false ones. There is another way that may appear to be simpler, easier and more elementary, but in reality it is of a higher nature. That is, do not be afraid of vicious visions, nor delighted with pleasing and tempting ones. Keep a kind heart, be aboveboard and calm. Everything will come to pass. You may see the Bodhisattva descending on you, or the Buddha accepting you as a disciple. These are false images, created by the Maya. When talking about visions, there is really no difference between that of the Buddha or Maya. They are illusory, too. Do not be dismayed if you see the devil. No need to be overjoyed to see the Buddha, either. Only by getting rid of illusions can we attain the truly advanced level of qigong.

Some qigong practitioners may also hear voices. The voices may be one or more; sometimes it is male or female. Some voices are pleasant and help people solve difficult problems. Some are frightening and constantly follow the person. These practitioners may feel puzzled and won't know what to do.

Exactly what is this kind of voice? In plain terms, voices and visions are the same thing. While vision is formed with the sense of seeing, voice is an image formed with the sense of hearing. The way we handle the voices, therefore, should not be any different from the way we handle the visions. First of all, sort out the real from the false. I wrote about a qigong master, Zhang Weixiang, who heals large numbers of sick people with the help of a benign voice. Mostly the voices that brag about things or threaten people are bogus. It is important to make distinctions.

Another way to deal with voices is to pay no attention and they will simply vanish after some time. There is no need to be stuck or frightened by these voices. We Chinese have a saying, "If one remains calm upon seeing strange things, the strangeness will do no harm." This can be applied to the kind of strange or unusual things that sometimes come along in our practice. Since there are visions and voices, we can infer that there are other forms such as smell, feel or taste, and sometimes certain psychological reactions. When dealing with these, the above-mentioned principle can be a frame of reference.

Some practitioners of Fragrance qigong are very enthusiastic about the pleasant fragrance they smell during practice. This is wrong. Smelling fragrance means nothing in terms of attainment. Besides, there is also the distinction of real fragrance or imaginary. At the advanced state of practice, this should not be the goal one seeks.

In particular, we must understand that illusions, be they seeing, hearing, smelling, or other physical or psychological reactions, are a natural stage in our practice. We must keep our minds free from delusion and resistance. The key is to keep a true heart and maintain serenity. If we obstinately hold on to superficial signs, we run the risk of falling into pitfalls and taking the wrong path.

Qigong and Healing

The conventional healing process is the first step in qigong healing, and we must pay special attention to the following aspects: the patient's natural environment, social environment, background, work, life, family, present circumstances, physical and psychological conditions, as well as dietary habits and medical history. In order to heal a patient, it is important to know the person so as to help him or her in the readjusting process.

In some cases, a change of place may be all that's needed. In others, we may help the patient make some adjustment to the social environment. Some may need counseling, while others may need psychiatric therapy. Regulating dietary intake may be sufficient in some cases, while in others medication must be used. Also, direct medical procedures such as surgery can be employed.

If a practitioner happens to be a medical doctor, he or she will almost certainly understand the need for diagnosing the overall conditions of the patient.

Qigong and Healing: Intuition

A higher level of qigong healing has to do with intuition. Experienced doctors rarely rely exclusively on their medical knowledge and logical reasoning. They "feel" things. Such intuitive feeling enables doctors to make a correct judgment in a moment. They may choose treatments that appear to be strange yet are surprisingly effective.

I am acquainted with a doctor of Traditional Chinese Medicine who is known for his ability to heal mental disturbance. He once had a young woman patient. She was suffering from stomach swelling and believed that her belly was full of snakes, having once drunk water from a bucket and found some tiny worms on the bottom. She had visited many large hospitals and was told by doctors that she was all right; there was nothing wrong and it was ridiculous to think she had snakes in her stomach. She would not listen, and her stomach became bigger each day. After my doctor friend took over the case, he decided to tell her that surgery was to be performed. He also made some arrangement with her family members. On the day of the surgery, the patient was put on an operating table. The doctor began the surgery by cutting a small opening on the outer skin of her stomach, meanwhile making sure the woman could see the process from a mirror nearby. He quickly took several little snakes from a bucket and showed them to the patient, telling her they were taken out of her stomach. He then sewed the cutting back. After the "surgery," the young woman was cured. Her stomach swelling disappeared, and she was not troubled any more. This was a very special kind of psychiatric treatment. The doctor, using intuition, decided on the treatment while talking with the patient.

If when treating patients doctors are able to keep their minds in a relaxed and tranquil state, they often can find treatment with miraculous results.

Qigong and Healing: Psychic Healing

The highest level of qigong healing is psychic healing—cures that use paranormal power as a medium. In recent years, such cases have become more and more common among practitioners of qigong. Many have been documented and can be verified. Some examples include instant healing of a bone fracture and curing tumors with mental command.

How to Develop Supernormal Healing Powers

Besides improving their own health, some qigong practitioners hope to develop some form of supernormal healing power. Personally I do not see anything wrong with this goal.

How can we develop and nurture our healing power? More often than not, qigong practitioners do not realize they possess healing power until they encounter some kind of emergency situation such as the serious condition of a relative's or friend's health, or seeing an accident on the road. Under such circumstances the practitioner may find no other help and has to go it alone, and unexpectedly, the person is healed.

Do not think the power comes to the practitioner by accident. He or she already has it without knowing it. As a matter of fact, every one of us, by nature, possesses the power to heal; how much that power is developed depends on how much we have nurtured it consciously. The majority of us never have the chance to expand the power within us.

If you are practicing qigong and would like to help people, you may decide to begin trying out your healing power. Do not be too concerned with success. My observation is that as long as a person is willing to try, he or she can call up some form of healing ability. Willingness is an important aspect of developing one's power. Once you do obtain certain healing power, how can you enhance and improve it?

Secret One:
Freedom From Anxiety

The number one rule for enhancing one's healing power is to free oneself from any anxiety. Harbor no vainglory. Just do it. I have seen many highly adept qigong masters underperform themselves. The reason is simply that their minds were not "empty."

In contrast, I have also seen quite a few young boys with psychic abilities who are not concerned with being successful. As a result, their healing powers improve more quickly.

There are yet others who had strong and effective healing power when they were young, but as they got older, lost the power. Undoubtedly this involves a lot of reasons, not the least of which is increased concern with saving face when their minds are anything but "empty."

Secret Two:
Compassion and Love

Compassion and love play a significant role in healing. More than one healer has described the same puzzling experience: in the healing process, sometimes they do very well with some kind of diseases, while for others they can do nothing. And when they perform healing on patients with the same disease, often they can cure one patient but not the other, regardless how much they try. They wonder why.

Of course we know that qigong healing is not a cure-all. It is not strange that some ailments are beyond the power of qigong masters, and there is nothing wrong with that. But why does it happen that working with different patients with the same disease can have such dramatic inconsistencies? The reason is actually very simple. It has a lot to do with the subtle impression of the patient on the healer. In the case of the patient for whom the qigong master immediately feels some kind of empathy and desire to help, the healer does not have to consciously transmit qi and the patient is healed.

Sometimes the healer does not feel any connection to the patient but still the work has to be done. Under such circumstances, no matter how hard the healer may try, the healing result cannot be good.

We all know that healing power, including qigong healing, is not something one can attain with logical reasoning. It is a kind of latent power which is especially subject to the influence of the subconscious.

If a healer follows certain standards in selecting patients, his attitude toward them will be different. If he feels compassion for a patient, the effect of healing will become obvious. If he takes a dislike to a patient, albeit unconsciously, his subconscious mind will then react against the healing effort and the result will not be effective.

Therefore, let us keep in mind that although there are many techniques for improving one's healing power, whether for high adept or common practitioner, we should never forget the simplest yet most fundamental rule: be compassionate and loving. Like any other medical profession, psychic healing must include compassion. Compassion is also instrumental to enhancing healing power.

Secret Three:
Be Flexible

Qigong healing should not be confined to one method or restricted to one style. There are a lot of ways and means to paranormal healing. It is essential to be flexible and use whatever ways work to get the best healing results. The goal is one: to heal. It is better to use our potentials to the fullest and never get into a rut by sticking to conventions.

When treating tumors through qigong healing, some qigong masters accomplish a cure by channeling qi. Others use their hands to grasp at the diseased part. Still others grasp in the air and then rub their own hands to cause the tumor to disappear. One is as effective as the other. Bear in mind that different techniques can be used to heal, whether they are acupuncture, acupressure, massage, and so forth. Use them as long as they work. You do not have to stick to any one established practice or accustomed rule. On the other hand, if you have a certain method that has been proven efficacious, use it and use it well. In other words, keeping an open mind and having no prohibitions help to enhance the healing power.

Secret Four:
Patient's Participation

Although it is important to get the patient to participate in the healing process, at times when it is unnecessary or impossible to have the patient's cooperation, such as when the patient is unconscious or is an infant, the healing can be just as effective. And in spite of the distrust of a patient, a qigong healer can still cure a fracture in seconds, instantly remove a tumor or get a paralytic to stand and walk. Usually a healer must have very strong power to be able to do this, but it shows that qigong healing is powerful and effective, independent of a patient's will.

In many cases, however, a patient's participation and cooperation are essential to effecting the healing result. It is important, then, to be able to get the patient into the required state, and synchronize the energy flow of both the sender of qi and the receiver.

Secret Five:
Faith and Confidence

It may seem simple, but faith and confidence are essential to healing. Above all, we must have confidence that man does have the power to heal and that we ourselves are also blessed with such power. Many records bear proof to the fact that paranormal healing has cured many diseases. Your healing ability is, to a large extent, dependent on your confidence, which is also the basis for further enhancement. As your healing power becomes more and more effective, you will have more and more confidence in your power. It is a process of compliment and supplement, through which your healing powers are nurtured and improved.

You can try this and the other principles we have discussed and you will begin to show some degree of healing power. For those possessing one form or another of healing power, more can be developed. It sometimes happens, however, that you help a patient heal but he denies that qigong had anything to do with it; he insists that it is his medication that finally worked. When you run into such a fellow, do not argue, but maintain the confidence that your healing works. Have no doubt about your healing power. Continue to help people, and before long you will find your own healing power becoming stronger and stronger. It is very important to be positive and confident. That is the basic of the basics.

Qigong and Paranormal
Sensory Perception

Paranormal sensory perception is a part of psychic power.

This category includes clairvoyance, telergy, telepathy and prediction, and so forth. With some training, anyone who possesses paranormal sensory perception can easily develop the ability to heal. On the other hand, those who have healing powers can also be trained to develop some form of extra sensory perception. Usually persons having strong healing power can also hope to transform their power into some kind of telekinetic ability.

The Key to Developing Psychic Power

Many people believe that psychic power is highly mysterious and are fascinated by it. In order to increase your interest as well as give you some experience of so-called psychic power, I am going to talk a little about how to develop the power of prediction. If you find it interesting, you may want to try it out in your qigong practice.

This method is derived from one of the secret instructions of qigong. For those practitioners who have attained a more advanced level, many can start from here and gradually nurture their psychic power.

These are the steps to developing psychic power:

Step 1: Select an object for prediction;

Step 2: Define your movements, designating yes and no;

Step 3: Get into the qigong state;

Step 4: Ask your question;

Step 5: Get into a deeper state of qigong;

Step 6: Wait for the answer.

The second step may need some explanation: by defining movements, we designate a particular move affirmative or negative. For instance, nodding of head means yes, shaking of head means no.

When you are ready, quiet down and get into your usual

qigong state. Then ask your question, such as whether the weather
will change and begin snowing tomorrow. After the question, concentrate again and wait to see if your body responds with a nod or
a shake of the head. Remember, every act is natural and uncon-
trolled. See how your body improvises.

If the question is somewhat more complex, you may need
to subgroup the answers. For example, if you want to know when
it may snow today, you could first ask, "Will it snow in the morning?" The answer may be "yes" or "no." "Yes" means it will snow
in the morning, and "no" means in the afternoon. If you knew it
was to be in the afternoon, you could begin to get more specific: If
you ask "Will it be at one o'clock?" the question would be followed
by "yes" or "no." If "no," continue until you get the final answer.

In the beginning, try not to predict things that have a close
relationship with yourself because subjective desires are usually
involved in such cases. When you strongly wish something to be
successful, it may often happen to the contrary. On the other hand,
in your prediction you may consciously or unconsciously cause
your head to nod if such is your wish, and thus the result can be
misleading.

After some training, you may start making predictions about
things that relate to yourself, but try to refrain from doing so at the
outset. It is easy to make mistakes when your welfare is too closely
involved. And the more mistakes you make, the less you become
confident in your ability to predict.

First try to predict something that has no direct impact on
your own interests or experience. In such a way, your subconscious
mind can be called on to work without too much interference and
distraction.

Second, try to predict things that are not familiar to you. For
instance, maybe you are a doctor and are really not knowledge-
able about economics. When you predict economic growth, your

consciousness is not restricted and your mind is empty. Your unconscious mind will give answers. When you must predict things that you know a great deal about, be guarded against misrepresentations of subjective wishes or past experience.

Above all, we must remember that there is no need to seek out psychic power. The predicting method I laid out above is only a way to enlighten your perceptual understanding, to show that there is no mystery in psychic ability. Hopefully, more people will understand qigong and human paranormal power through this demonstration.

Trouble is Bodhi (Enlightenment)

Whether they practice qigong or not, all human beings are sometimes troubled by worries. Somehow it seems we just cannot get away from them.

Qigong practitioners all know that a good environment and tranquil mind are essential to their practice. Unfortunately those fundamentals are sometimes unreachable. Relating to family, work, children, parents, and co-workers distracts us, and there seems to be no end to problems of all kinds. How are we supposed to keep up an efficient practice?

A lot of practitioners ask me about being distracted; it is obviously a real and common problem in our practice. To be honest, I am an extremely optimistic person myself, but all too often troubles and worries besiege me. All I can say is that troubles and problems are good—very good—for a qigong practitioner. If one has no worries or problems bothering him, it is a handicap. Trouble is Bodhi, and it provides the best challenge to our determination to overcome it.

How, then, do we overcome problems? Sometimes when we are troubled by something, we tell ourselves to ignore it, not to be bothered by it. We try to suppress it. But that will not help and things may get worse. I have talked about the principle of "conquer without conquering" in my discussion of concentration, substituting ten thousand thoughts with one thought. When you are troubled by something, try to find your "true self," your "original self," and look at the trouble through the eye of your true self. Analyze how your mind is being troubled and make no conscious effort to stop it. Try to experience it. Gradually, you may be able, through your true self, to experience this process: your mind is so troubled that it tosses and turns like the rolling ocean, one wave surging after another. Try to stay calm and collected, standing aloof and observing. Suddenly, the tide falls. Those of us who have experienced such a moment know that when the tide of unrest falls, the mind is in such a peaceful state that it is more thrilling than the relaxing state of qigong we have talked about. Once we overcome the troubled mind, our practice is improved too.

We also know that it is easier to stay calm in a quiet environment, while it is more difficult to maintain tranquillity in trouble. It requires a higher level of attainment. We may easily enter the state of qigong when we are free and relaxed. Nevertheless, we can achieve greater advances when we are peaceful and free in times of trouble.

Free of All Restrictions

What should we know about qigong practice and what principles should we follow? First, discard practices that narrow and restrict our development. We need to view qigong from a macro perspective rather than look at it as a set of regulated routine movements or enshroud it in mystery. It is important that practitioners of qigong, through their practice, become more adjusted to modern life, more flexible in solving life's problems and more efficient in carrying out their life's missions. We should be free of all restrictions to attain higher levels of practice.

A large number of scientists and scholars claim they do not take qigong seriously. That is fine. It takes time for the majority of people to accept and understand certain things. It is unnecessary to rush this process.

In China, as elsewhere, some people regard qigong as fraudulent. Admittedly, fraudulent qigong does exist. By acknowledging this, the vanguard role that qigong plays in the science of the future cannot be diminished.

In modern society, man is confronted with so many unsettling factors. Many people suffer from physical or mental ailments. If you are told that there is a form of self-cultivation that promises well-being for both body and mind, as long as you understand it correctly, master it efficiently and use it wisely, why would you refuse? It can help you be more flexible in life and more tolerant of yourself and others.

The mystery of qigong, the mystery of human paranormal power, as well as the mysteries of all human metaphysical phenomena, once unraveled, will cause the sciences of man to be rewritten. Human civilization and intelligence will be raised to new levels. Qigong is a phenomenon in itself, providing a way for us to readjust both our physical bodies and our spiritual awareness. It offers us a gateway to a whole new sphere of human life.

It is my belief that our efforts today will become invaluable in the 21st century. May every one of us find more and more new experience in our qigong practice.

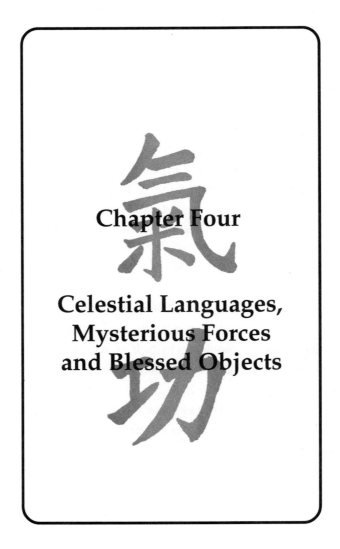

Chapter Four

Celestial Languages, Mysterious Forces and Blessed Objects

About Celestial Languages

Quite a number of readers have written to me about a phenomenon they encountered in their qigong practice: voices were involuntarily uttered from their mouths in a strange tongue that nobody could understand. I myself have observed a number of such occurrences. In qigong, this is generally termed "celestial languages."

Many qigong practitioners speak one kind or another of such celestial languages, and they are all different from each other. Most speakers of celestial language know nothing about what is being uttered. Some claimed to understand it but were proven to be entirely ignorant of the true meaning of the strange tongue. There are, however, some practitioners who are able to translate the celestial languages. A few people have written about this phenomenon, believing that these languages contain certain messages from the universe and belong to beings of higher wisdom. I also know of someone who can converse in celestial languages.

Celestial Languages and Their Functions

What, then, are celestial languages? Are they worthy of our attention, and in what ways?

Usually, celestial language begins to emerge when the practitioner is in the state of qi. It seems to be completely different from any human language, composed of a series of syllables that are incomprehensible to most people, even beyond the comprehension of the speaker.

Celestial languages seem to be non-repeatable. One person may describe his or her feeling toward a certain subject in one celestial language. If asked to do the same thing again, the person generally is incapable of repeating it in the same language.

Because celestial languages are inconsistent, they lack the regularity, accuracy, as well as the compatibility and translatability of human language. As a result, many people who know nothing about such phenomena regard these as some sort of joke.

The utterance of celestial language may be accidental, but in most cases it is induced by a certain wish or desire on the part of the practitioner.

For some time, celestial language has been painted with a coat of mystifying color, but in reality it does have certain special effects and functions that serve practical purposes.

What are the functions of celestial language? First of all, self-adjustment—it seems to have an adjusting effect on those who utter such language, enabling them to get into the so-called state of qi, or deepen such a state. It also helps induce others to enter the state of qi. It can help transmit qigong skills by inducing the practitioner into the state of qi, so it is one way to pass on the ability of the master.

Celestial language has the capacity to affect a person's physical and mental state, which often manifests in the form of curing diseases.

Celestial language contains certain cosmic messages. Some practitioners use celestial language to express their impressions or feelings about a certain person or phenomenon, and oftentimes these expressions contain a form of prediction. Because it contains certain messages, it can be translated into human languages. Of course such translation is not a literal translation as it is between human languages, but a form of free translation without corresponding verbiage that can nevertheless convey the message being transmitted. In fact, any translation, even between languages, is a form of conveying meanings rather than exchanging languages.

In this sense, celestial language does not have a set of rules with which we can analyze and study it. To translate it, the translator needs to possess the extraordinary ability to understand such a language.

The Nature and Mystery of the Celestial Languages

It is very important to differentiate between the celestial language phenomena that are sometimes claimed by qigong practitioners. We must understand that of the many celestial languages, most are nonsensical and useless, and it would be ridiculous to be mesmerized by them.

What are the secrets of functional celestial language? First, in terms of the nature of celestial languages, it is a form of spontaneous movement of the vocal system in the body once it enters the state of qi. Here I must emphasize that it should be actual involuntary movement. As a matter of fact, any form of complete involuntary bodily movement in the state of qi has a certain functional effect, be it vocal sound or body movement, which can affect others through various sensual organs and with certain rhythms.

Rhythm can be seen as a program of life. Just as different musical genres affect the audience's physical and psychological reaction in different ways, the spontaneous movements in the state of qi have similar capacities. The secret of transmitting qigong through celestial language lies right here.

The various movements, even painting and calligraphy, can be seen as a form of dancing, while celestial language may be regarded as a form of singing, all with the capacity of self-adjusting, affecting others, curing diseases and transmitting qigong.

A person possesses such power when completely in the state

of qigong because he or she truly lets go of all restrictions and relaxes, and every part of the body regains its natural state. All intellectual and logical perceptions give way to the original mind. The
unconscious takes over, acting without action. In such a state, the
unconscious is readjusting and reformulating one's body and mind.
This is a process with its own extraordinary programming and
methodology, and is so complex as to be beyond our human understanding and interpretation. In this process, a series of rhythms
are created, either in the form of body movement or vocal sound,
which cause the entire physical body and mental state to be in a
special programming system. Celestial language, being one of these
programming systems, is more than simple vocal exercise but con-
veys an inner rhythm through which one's body and mind are at-
tuned with the universe.

　　In our daily life, we are constantly in a distorted state. Once
we are liberated from all the man-made rules, intellectual pursuits,
profit calculations, and other so-called normal thinking processes,
the natural and harmonious rhythm of our original vital life force
is released and starts its intuitive readjustment of our body and
mind. That is the secret of nature.

　　When we are entirely merged in such a spontaneous state,
and involuntarily start uttering certain vocal sounds, or making
certain body movements, it is a way to self-adjust the body and
spirit. We can also affect others through our rhythmic movements.
Other people, especially those sensitive and trusting souls who
are free of psychological inhibitions, will be affected through their
sensual organs and become harmonized by these repeated rhythms.

　　Using this as a starting point, we may also imagine that all
forms of existence in the universe are connected, not only man
and heaven but also other of nature's life forms. One of the connections is this rhythmic programming, which can be perceived
by every life form. Music, rhythm, movement, all can have an ef-

fect not only on man but on animals and plants as well. For example, parents sing a lullaby to their baby so it can go to sleep. Farmers play music to cows in order to produce more milk. Gardeners play music to the flowers so they bloom earlier and better. All these prove the fact that all things and beings in the universe are connected, man and heaven, life and non-life, everything and all things.

The entire universe—the sun, the moon and the stars, rivers, lakes, oceans, mountains and fields—all have their rhythms, their songs and dances. This enormous dancing rhythm is constantly exerting its effect on the universe: man, animal and plant, who also have their songs and dances. All these inner rhythms are connected and interplaying. When one is entirely in a natural state, his rhythm must be open to connection with the universe.

We experience a great deal of differences in our daily lives. Personality differences often prevent us from seeing any likeness between humans, not to mention the differences between human and animal, animal and plant, and non-life forms. Nevertheless, once one enters the state of qi, without any help of language or other conventional communication forms, one will experience that missing connection between all things. Many scientific experiments have shown that in the state of qi, man can affect plants or animals through sheer mind force. Such force can also directly affect non-life objects. The deeper one gets into the state of qi, the easier it is to become connected with other people or other objects, in harmony with heaven and earth, unraveling the secret of universal connection.

Celestial Messages and Prediction

My theory of human physio-cosmology recognizes that the human unconscious is all-knowing and prevailing. However, it is next to impossible to convert the unconscious knowing to conscious understanding, and convey it in normal language. There is an almost insurmountable barrier between the unconscious and the conscious.

So-called psychic perception or prediction is in reality the ability to raise the all-knowing power of the unconscious and make it into conscious knowing. That makes all the difference: when a person's unconscious remains buried, he does not have the power. When he can bring it to the foreground of consciousness, we say he possesses the power of psychic perception.

Usually, when one encounters a person or an object, one's unconscious perception has already received all the messages. Once one enters into the state of qi, such messages are revealed without the interference of the thinking process, and doesn't need the medium of movement or language. What results is the all-knowing judgment of the unconscious, which is without errors. Under such circumstances, no intellect, no logic, no conscious thinking is involved. There is only intuitive feeling, which carries through the judgment of the unconscious.

How is the intuitive feeling translated into a language that can be processed by the conscious mind? It often happens in qigong practice that a practitioner, in the state of qi, expresses his perception and prediction about a certain person or happening through celestial language. The practitioner may not be able to translate his own celestial language. However, there may be somebody who heard what he said and translated it. In this way, the process is complete; that is, the psychic perception is accomplished. In this case, it took two individuals to finish the process. The translator who was able to convey what had been said into something more intelligible obviously also possessed a certain degree of psychic ability. He lacked the power of direct perception, but his psychic ability is transformed into his perception of the celestial language.

Sometimes a person has a very strong supernatural perception and his unconscious mind can access all the information in a person or an object, and immediately transfer it into something similar to celestial language. It is simply because human unconsciousness is all knowing and celestial language is the most elementary manifestation of the prediction ability of the unconscious.

Celestial Language is Nothing Mysterious

Having discussed the functions of celestial languages, it is necessary to point out that not all of them spoken by qigong practitioners have the same prediction power, just as many of the so-called spontaneous movements in the state of qi are not spontaneous in that they are mostly the result of the subjective wish of some practitioners. When practitioners force themselves to achieve the ability of such things as spontaneous movement or celestial language, they get nothing.

Like other spontaneous movements, celestial language is not at all mysterious, but it has certain potential risks. For mentally unstable persons or people with a history of mental illness, blind pursuit of the so-called celestial languages will almost certainly cause mental disturbance. There have been many instances like this. While some people thought they possessed supernatural power, it was really deviation. So, do not pursue it.

The Mysterious Force Behind Psychic Ability

In my research of qigong, human psychic power and supernatural phenomena, I often come across a mystifying power that lies behind them. It is always this mysterious power that creates many incredibly miraculous phenomena. On one hand, this force manifests itself in the form of high level qigong skills and mysterious supernatural powers. On the other hand, it also becomes the source of some people's suffering.

Subjective Personality

In my book, *Decoding Human Metaphysical Phenomena,* I wrote about Mr. Wang Youcheng from Jilin Province, who is well-known for his supernatural abilities. I have made very careful studies of Wang's psychic claims. In the past years, he has also given many demonstrations to many audiences both at home and abroad. In addition, he coordinated experiments and lab tests, many with several scientific research institutions. His extra sensory perception (ESP) and psychokinetic ability have been proven by many replicable scientific tests.

In my research and investigation, I observed that whenever Wang Youcheng gave a demonstration, he always entered a state of total relaxation and tranquillity. He maintained a complete sense of self, without any alien personality interfering. He kept clear control of himself.

But he also wrote a book entitled *Who Am I?.* Clearly, even though Wang has complete control of his sense of self and feels no intervention from any obvious source, he still experiences a certain intervention from a mysterious force beyond his grasp.

Wang once told me that when he first heard of someone's telekinetic ability, he wanted very much to have the same power. He tried but never succeeded. One day while dozing he suddenly saw in his dream an old man holding a bottle of pills, making some gesture to show him how to get pills from the bottle without breaking the seal. All of a sudden he woke up and grabbed a pill bottle on the coffee table and did what the old man showed him in the dream. He did it, and since then he has been able to remove pills from sealed bottles. During the first months of his new-found power, he showed everyone who was willing to witness his demonstration, feeling both excited and awed, wondering whether what he had been doing was real or not. He told me, "No wonder people have a hard time believing in psychic powers. I was so full of doubt myself during those first months, even after I acquired such power. It is simply too far-removed from our normal human experience."

In China, there are quite a number of others who have somewhat similar abilities as that of Wang Youcheng, differing in degrees and including both qigong practitioners and non-practitioners. They all have a very clear sense of self, never losing control of their conscious mind. In qigong practice as well as in the realm of human psychic powers, paranormal ability belongs to the most wholesome.

Power from
Invisible Masters

In China, the media has provided considerable coverage of the psychic Mr. Zhang Baosheng and I have no intention of retelling his stories. Generally speaking, although Zhang also maintains good control of himself, he appears to be always in a state of trance. In his daily activities, he is more often than not absentminded. He said once that he would sometimes see an old man with a white beard whom he believed to be his invisible master. Some close acquaintances of Zhang revealed that when doing certain psychic demonstrations he would ask for instructions from his master.

Who is this invisible master? Is it a creation of the imagination, of the unconscious mind? Or is it some form of intervention from the unknown? It certainly gives much cause for reflection.

Again, some qigong practitioners' claims of seeing certain images are not necessarily fictitious. They may indeed envisage some kind of images, along with which certain forms of psychic abilities emerge.

Direct Control
from Invisible Masters

We all know that the human unconscious holds in store enormous energies. Usually, however, we cannot force our unconscious mind to work. In China, we have an old saying which is "to pay respect to gods and seek advice." We have to be respectful to get effective assistance.

Whether qigong practitioners demonstrate high level qigong feats, or psychics maneuver the supernatural powers, it is necessary that they go through certain operating processes, which among insiders is termed "seeking the master." The demonstrator needs to "seek the master for advice," and then he may set a goal and get into that state of total relaxation, leaving himself to chance and awaiting the emergence of his power. At such a time we may see various forms of psychic abilities, such as psychokinesis, ESP healing, telekinesis, and so on.

In the case described above, the "master" does not usually have a clear-cut personality or form. It may not manifest in the form of sound or visual image, either. Neither the practitioner nor the psychic is under the control of an alien entity. He only needs to say a certain prayer and the power will come to him. The psychic healer Shen Chang, whom we met in the previous chapter, is one of these, and he uses the same method when he performs healing.

The "master" may be understood as our true spirit, that mysterious force stored in the depth of our unconscious. On the other hand, certain messages from the universe may also be understood as coming from the external.

The Positive Power of Sound

In *Decoding Human Metaphysical Phenomena* I also wrote about Wu Jaing, a qigong practitioner with supernatural healing powers. His extraordinary ability comes from a sound, a vocal image formed through years of qigong and similar practices. The sound talks to him, instructs him and answers questions for him. Eventually the sound gave him the power of healing. There are many cases such as this among qigong practitioners or psychic healers.

In his own opinion, Wu Jiang believes that the sound comes from some other celestial bodies. In much of our research and experiments, we feel that it is more likely that this sound has its origin in his unconscious, and has acquired a certain independent form of existence. Wu Jiang's psychic healing power undoubtedly is largely related to the sound, a supernatural existence. It is a positive relationship, and instead of being disturbed by it, Wu Jiang has benefited a great deal from this relationship.

The Negative Power of Sound

Those of you who have read *Decoding Human Metaphysical Phenomena* should all know the case of Jin Quyi. Out of curiosity, he first tried consulting oracles, and later acquired the ability of automatic writing. Finally he began to hear sounds and see visions, which gained control over him.

Such cases often involve a certain special process. It may be because the person has undergone tremendous psychological suffering and lost his mental balance. It may also be that erroneous qigong practice caused a negative effect. Under such circumstances a sound or vision will form an abnormal personality and have control over the person. This often causes enormous mental anguish and suffering. The sound or vision will order, threaten and confuse the person. I have quite a number of readers who described to me the same experience in their letters. In a sense this can be a form of mental disorder. In the field of qigong practice and psychosis, it is a subject of special interest.

Possessed by an Alien Personality

Such cases usually occur when someone has undergone severe shock or accident, such as being hit by a lightning bolt, contracting a serious disease, or having an almost deadly accident. Perhaps the person lost consciousness and after coming around found himself or herself possessed by a certain alien personality. In such cases the possessed person normally maintains his own senses and personality. But the alien personality can manifest in the person through different ways. It may appear without being requested or upon request. Whenever the alien personality surfaces, the possessed will usually appear to transform into another person, and his or her facial expressions, accent, as well as pulse and blood pressure are dramatically altered. Sometimes a female will assume the voice of a male, and vice versa, or use dialects of other provinces that cannot have been known to the possessed. What is more, things or subjects being revealed are mostly beyond the knowledge or experiences of the person. It is obvious that there is a distinct personality existing inside the person. Alien personalities sometimes claim to be someone who has died long ago, in some cases centuries ago. Their existence can be verified by historical events they recount or by their knowledge of the time past. In certain cases, very young children will say something that only mature adults could have spoken, and likely these words have been from a person long gone.

Some alien personalities maintain a kind of positive relationship with the possessed, others negative. When doing research, we need to differentiate the situation.

Trance States

The most typical of the trance states, or temporary possession, can be seen in various sorcery practices existing in remote areas. When the need arises for special circumstances, such as driving away evil spirits or curing disease, the sorceress or sorcerer, an otherwise very normal and sane person, will suddenly enter a trance state, or completely lose consciousness, or be thrown into some kind of violent state. Muttering incantations, the person will claim to be a god or the ancestor of someone, in a voice other than his or her own. He or she would say things that are completely inconsistent with his or her knowledge, sometimes revealing things that happened generations back in someone's family. Generally, once the person regains consciousness, he or she has no memory at all of what has happened. It is like a dream forgotten. In such trance states, psychic healing or predictions can usually be accomplished.

The above are some cases of mysterious force at play. Although it may appear in varying forms, manifesting itself either in a positive or negative manner, lasting longer or shorter, some with sound or image and some without, its secrets can be unraveled by research into the deeper structure of human consciousness, and by study of the relations between humans and the universe.

About Blessed Objects

When talking about qigong, especially the recently emerged "Message Qigong," it is often necessary to speak of "blessed objects."

Is the thought of blessed objects really so mystifying? Do blessed objects contain any message; are they a result of psychological suggestion or are they simply nonsense? Let us say that blessed objects do have certain mysteries and their unraveling will not only deepen our understanding of the supreme essence of qigong, but also our understanding of man and the universe.

Blessed objects can be anything from a book, a scroll of calligraphy, a talisman, a banner, or any object that has been "blessed" by qigong masters, such as a watch, pen, necklace, ring, notebook, mirror, paper-weight, rosary beads, ink stand, food or drink. Once the objects are blessed by a qigong master, they contain certain "messages" that have an effect on other practitioners.

What are the secrets of blessed objects? There are several levels to help us understand their meaning.

First: Self-Suggestion

Although most qigong practitioners tend to deny this level of association, in my opinion it certainly does exist. For example, someone without any qualification "pretends" to be a qigong master, and gives you something that has been "blessed." You truly believe that it can give you the desired effect, that it can cure your ailment. So you take the object, which can be something to wear (a personal object such as a talisman), or some kind of offering; you may also eat or drink it if it is food. You trust beyond the shadow of a doubt that a miracle will occur, and indeed it does. That is the work of your self-suggestion.

But that is not all; the theory of self-suggestion is not the only explanation. From the viewpoint of qigong, it is a matter of faith, of belief; in other words, "sincerity begets miracles." Your faith and sincerity enable you to enter the state of qi, at which time your original self takes over and becomes the master. Everything then will be completed without your doing.

For example, a person goes to the temple to pray for something, or make confession. He is all sincerity, and he gets what he wants. We can credit this to the formula "sincerity begets miracles." There is no Buddha or bodhisattva. It is your own sincere belief, your faith, your wishing power. It is the Buddha nature in you, your original self, which in nature is all powerful. It is overshadowed by our worldly existence. In utter sincerity, your heart is purified and your mind is cleared, and that is when your Buddha nature starts to shine again.

If the blessed objects come from a genuine qigong master, again the implied message as well as your self-suggestion are equally effective.

The fact that an accomplished qigong master has many convincing abilities that are trusted and revered by others, and has built up authority through his or her abilities, all contribute to the effectual suggestive power over the sincere believers.

Good qigong practitioners are all effective in using various means of suggestions, and blessed objects is one of these.

Second: Willpower at Work

The effect of self-suggestion is not the only factor at work in the use of a blessed object. There are many such cases in which the patients recover immediately after taking food or drink blessed by the qigong master, even while the patients either have little faith or are extremely dubious of the healing power of qigong. It succeeds because generally speaking, once the object is blessed by the qigong master, it contains a certain message. When it is given to the recipient, the message starts to take effect. It may be said to play a symbolic role.

The kind of energy stored in blessed objects is not necessarily understood by using the theory of physics. The real secret is the transmission of willpower. For instance, the qigong master has transmitted energy to drinking water, which consequently becomes an object with healing messages. He hands the water to you, but in reality he is transmitting the willpower of healing. You take the water and drink it, but in reality you receive the willpower that cures your ailment. In this case, the water is not significant in and of itself. The process of willpower transmission, from the act of blessing the water, to handing over the water, to taking and drinking the water, is of great significance.

Not only drinking water, but other objects such as a watch,

after being blessed by the qigong master and given back to you to wear, can also carry the will power transmittal.

You may then ask why we need the object. Can we just transmit and receive the message? Well, we must understand that methods vary with transmission. There may be tens of thousands of ways to transmit, and blessed objects are among one of the most effective. Along with the object, the qigong master directs his healing energy through his willpower, and the patient can easily receive the energy.

The willpower itself needs a way to be mobilized and transmitted and these ways are many and varied. Blessed objects can be an effective way to bring out the healing message and transmit it to the recipient.

The secret of qigong healing is simply to use the most convenient and effective way to mobilize our willpower and get the message across.

Some of you may also ask if a blessed object carries the message of the willpower, will it have a long-lasting effect? The answer may be that willpower transmission is something that happens in a fraction of a second, in a flash. At the same time, it can be something that transcends time and space. So in some sense the willpower directed to you by the qigong master in that moment will transcend the here and now and have an effect that lasts all your life. The more you believe in this, the longer the effect will last. This is certainly not something that can be accomplished by mere self-suggestion.

Third: Physical Messages

Aside from the effects of self-suggestion from willpower transmission, the objects can be tested to see if there has been a transformation in their physical composition.

For example, after the qigong master has transmitted his

energy into a glass of water, is its compound changed? The fact that it has been changed has been proven more than once by scientists using highly controlled testing measurement.

We cannot help associating this with blessed objects. In the case of the water, once the energy has been transmitted, its physical compound has undergone a certain change. It is seen to have contained the message sent by the qigong master. The water is then handed to the recipient, who accepts and drinks it. It is possible that besides the effect of self-suggestion and thought transmission, there are also physical as well as biological effects that can be directly observed and described.

The many miraculous qigong feats and human supernatural phenomena are yet to be understood and explained by modern physics or biology. In the same vein, modern science has yet to explain the state and transmission of psychic messages and thought energy.

Fourth: Programmed Messages

In addition to direct energy transmission, other objects such as books, calligraphy and paintings can also effect transmission of thought energy. A person with abilities can transfer his energy or thought message through books or works of art.

This may be the result of suggestion or self-suggestion. It may also be the effect of thought energy transmission since the author's purpose is to get his or her message across to readers through his or her work. In the process, this thought message is sent out and at the time we read the book or see the art object, we also receive the message transmitted along with it.

Furthermore, we may speculate that the original piece of art or literary work may also contain direct physical energy that affects the reader or audience. To an adept, the process of artistic creation is also a state of transcendence. Naturally, his creative work, whether in language or art, consists of unique and special rhythms

which can be expressed in the abstract form of language or thinking, as well as in the tangible form of calligraphy or painting, the
rhythm of space and time. It is necessarily the product of his "state
of qi."

Therefore, when reading or appreciating a work of art created by such an adept in such a state, the rhythmic medium, be it
in the form of language or thinking, calligraphy or painting, would
be programmed in your heart and soul, thus arousing in you a
vibrating and synchronizing effect. Induced by the rhythm or program, you may enter into a state similar to that of the creator of the
work.

That is the secret imbedded in creative work such as books
or paintings. They constitute another level of energy transmission
once they are transformed into blessed objects. Thus revealed, we
can stop to ponder the mysterious efficacies of the amulet or talisman in qigong, as well as occult history.

To summarize, all blessed objects more or less fall into one
or more of the above categories of message and energy transmission.

All things under heaven may appear to be mystifying when
they are not understood. On the other hand, once we unravel the
mystery, they seem rather obvious.

Chapter Five

Eliminating Pitfalls
in Qigong Practice

Harbor No Enmity

All too often in our dealings with other people we tend to judge their intelligence. We say one person is clever and another is not so clever. The truth is, one's cleverness only surfaces in one's consciousness, while our human soul—our unconscious mind— shares the same wisdom that is all-knowing. When a person has a kind heart, the slowest witted will feel it. When a person harbors evil, an infant in his mother's arms will refuse his embrace. In our daily life, we sometimes come across one who appears to be bright and intelligent, a good actor on the stage of human drama. However, his hypercritical character may be discerned easily by somebody who may not be intelligent but whose subconscious mind can feel it immediately.

Those who truly understand the essence of qi gong must not look upon nature or other fellow human being as enemies. This may sound odd. Indeed, who would want to antagonize nature or other people? Well, as a matter of fact, it has a much deeper meaning than it sounds.

Say for example that today is a cold day. You do not like it at all, and as soon as you step out the door you curse the weather. What is this other than antagonism to nature? Tomorrow is going to be hot, and that is not your favorite, either. You blame the heat wave. What is this if not enmity toward nature? Even such seemingly innocent reactions to natural weather changes hinder your being one with heaven, being harmonious with nature. Regardless of how diligently you practice, and how constantly you remind yourself to be one with heaven and earth, it is just not going to work.

Similarly, in your contact with other people, you dislike this one and are jealous of that one, and are vigilant against the other one. You constantly put up all kinds of masks, trying to be all but yourself: trying to be authoritative, to be solemn, to be cultivated, to be humorous. In a strict sense, this is enmity toward others because you cannot look upon others as the same as yourself. You constantly guard against and keep your distance from others, and this prevents you from maintaining a tranquil mental state. Therefore, it does not matter what school of qigong you are practicing, because you are far from its practicing fundamentals.

A true qigong practitioner should, under whatever circumstance, consciously stay in a state of qi. It must be a genuine one, not one you are so often told to imagine yourself in, which brings you far short of the high level. What is the high level? It is that genuine feeling of compassion and loving kindness toward our fellow beings, that sense of connectedness with everyone, anyone.

We have repeatedly said that all ways return to the root, to the origin, and all ways lead to the One. What is the origin? What is the One?

When doing various qigong routines, many practitioners experience spontaneous movements induced by the circulating qi. When this happens, oftentimes even though you may be near other objects such as trees, rocks or iron fences, your movements will intuitively guide your body in such a way that, no matter how complex and unusual your movements may be, your body will not be hit or injured.

Once you are in a truly relaxed state, your original mind will take over and take care of everything. We live in nature and we live in society. As long as we maintain harmony with heaven and earth, as long as we harbor no enmity against others, and as long as our whole body and mind are in a state of tranquillity and peace, we can naturally handle our relations with the environment and people. We certainly will be balanced, mentally and physically.

When we genuinely feel a loving kindness toward nature and men, we are already in a natural state of relaxation. We will be free and easy. That is when enlightenment dawns.

Our practicing qigong must give us more freedom in life, make us feel more at ease with ourselves and enable us to understand more of the Zen philosophy. What is the point if we practice hard twenty-four hours a day but still feel harassed by worries and enjoy not a moment of relaxation?

In China today, qigong has become widely practiced. As more and more people begin to recognize the benefits of qigong and engage in its practice, we need to broadcast the positive significance of qigong and encourage all people to enjoy healthy growth. At the same time, to promote positive and wholesome development and bring qigong research to a higher level that will benefit more practitioners, it is extremely important to avoid the pitfalls existing in our movement.

Avoiding the Pitfalls

In the nearly two decades that qigong has been experiencing a renaissance in China, it has undergone great development and the number of practitioners has increased at an amazing rate. More encouragingly, more and more scientific researchers are drawn to the field of qigong study. At the same time, quite a number of unhealthy tendencies have been detected in the movement.

First, within certain schools of qigong a form of factionalism has been growing which has proven to be a hindrance to their reputation and development. More than just a problem of organizational structure, it tends to restrict their practitioners in their overall spiritual development and becomes a block to attaining a higher level of practice.

Second, disharmony exists between different schools of practice. One school may regard its routines to be more superior than others. Such tendencies directly affect the promotion of qigong as a unified movement, creating considerable confusion and negativity among practitioners.

Third, some qigong schools and practitioners tend to overestimate and exaggerate the healing function of qigong. Without doubt, qigong entails certain healing powers but it is not a cure-all. Also, when we are not absolutely sure of the mechanism of qigong healing, we should be allowed to speculate, investigate and offer various explanations, but we should not make false statements that are not entirely true. Dishonest practitioners overstate their power of healing and do it deliberately. They may claim to have cured a hundred cases while in reality only one has been healed. This should be stopped.

Fourth, that qigong is beneficial to mankind is beyond doubt. When it starts to grow out of a cultural trend and seek its independent status in society, it cannot help but come up against the problem of how to sustain itself economically. We should not be afraid to point out that the development of qigong depends largely on healthy economics. However, as qigong encounters the modern market economy, it should impose on itself a more rigorous moral standard while following the conventional rules of modern economy, because the fundamental nature of qigong is moral and spiritual cultivation. At the same time, how to balance qigong promotion and its economic development is a matter of practical importance. While it may seem a simple, conventional business problem, it nevertheless requires a conscious choice that may decide the future of qigong development in China.

The current situation of qigong is a positive development, and it is important to maintain its moral standard, which is crucial to the moral and spiritual advancement of practitioners and people in general.

There are many schools of qigong in China, and each has its own unique characteristics. We should not challenge each other on methodology of practice, but promote each other in such a way that we make clear the strength and weakness of each and draw on each other's merits, thereby raising the level together.

Different qigong methods have their uniquenesses and therefore vary in effect. Generally speaking, a good practice routine that is both practical and popular tends to have the following characteristics:

(1) It is easy to follow and popularize. To use Zen terminology, it is ready-made. More complex and obscure forms are unsuitable for large numbers of practitioners from all walks of life.

(2) It is effective in readjusting one's physical health.

(3) It is effective in readjusting one's psychological health.

(4) It is effective in cultivating wisdom.

(5) It is effective in promoting the moral civilization in society, based on individual well being and the well being of the practitioner's interrelationship with others and society.

(6) It is harmonious with modern civilization. Qigong should not discriminate or disparage modern science and technology but should harmonize with them. At present, certain qigong schools play down the roles of modern science and regard qigong as the only cure for all. They want nothing to do with hospitals or modern medicine. They seem to have forgotten that if qigong does not integrate with the achievements of modern science and technology, it will lose its reliance on modern society and lose its rational standing.

(7) It should enable practitioners to start at a low level but eventually achieve a higher level of attainment.

(8) It should have no or few deviations.

The above eight points constitute the basic standards for popular qigong routines.

Deviations in Qigong

I have observed throughout my study that there are deviations in qigong practice, and some can cause serious dysfunction.

Some qigong enthusiasts and practitioners deny that qigong practice can cause deviating dysfunction. This is obviously not a scientific and objective view, nor is it realistic. It is unscientific to think that recognition of such deviations will cause qigong to lose its reputation. This is neither objective nor true.

Through the years, I have met large numbers of practitioners as well as received numerous letters from readers of my works. To be honest, I have observed and investigated quite a few cases of mental disturbance caused by the incorrect practice of qigong. Of course, it is a very small proportion compared to the number of qigong practitioners in China. But it is not negligible considering the relatively large number of practitioners throughout the country. A single case may cause serious concern by family members as well as by other practitioners. Pressure may then follow. It is obvious that it would be wiser to study it objectively rather than to cover it up.

In my work, *Decoding Human Metaphysical Phenomena*, I analyzed the true case of qigong deviation. A man by the name of Jin Quyi, who started by consulting folk oracles, was finally controlled by the voice and image of an alien force who proclaimed itself to be Emperor Pangu, the legendary creator of the universe in Chinese mythology. While explaining to Jin the human evolution process from the time of creation, this force levied extreme control over him. As soon as he doubted the power of this force, a voice in his mind would say, "I can make you motionless this very moment." Immediately Jin felt his limbs and body stop functioning. Interestingly, this self-claimed creator force also showed Jin the wonderful future world.

Jin Quyi has written a book based on his personal experience, which won quite a large readership and gained some following. I made a careful investigation into this case and found a lot of contradictions in Jin's claims and narration. On the one hand, in his confusing trance-like state, he did acquire certain psychic insight and senses, such as prediction. On the other hand, he was so painfully under the absolute control of the mysterious force and longed to be free from its dominance, that the blueprint of a beautiful new world supposedly demonstrated to him by the so-called creator force was no more than unrealistic wishful thinking on Jin's part. In the analysis of modern psychotherapy, especially in light of Freud's dream analysis, the answer to Jin's case is apparent. Since the publication of my work, quite a few readers wrote me to say that my analyses have given them a more realistic and objective measurement of Jin's claims.

Recently I received several letters from the United States of America. In one of these letters, an elderly Chinese woman told me that for many decades she had suffered from the control of a voice in her mind. She could not get rid of it, and was very agonized. She later immigrated to America, thinking that by so doing the controlling force would be left behind. That did not happen, however, and she was still bothered by the mysterious force. She wrote me in the hope that I could do something to relieve her suffering.

There are similar cases among some qigong practitioners. Some are bothered, some are exulted, believing they are receiving instructions from celestial beings or from past masters such as Lao Tzu and Buddha. These are all the result of deviation from qigong practice, and our practitioners must distinguish it under the correct guidance of qigong masters.

Why do such deviations occur in qigong practice? We all know that the basic requirement of qigong practice is relaxation. In our daily life, we must constantly put ourselves under the control of reason and intellect. When we relax we relieve ourselves from this control. In such a process, it is possible that one's potential wisdom and positive energy is awakened or released. At the same time, other elements in our unconscious mind may be let loose too, such as one's suppressed desires, worries, fears and so forth. We may recall that in many guided qigong seminars given throughout the country by famous masters, many in the audience enter the spontaneous movement state and cry or scream. Why? They were releasing their suppressed feelings. It is normal in qigong practice to let loose one's unconscious and suppressed emotions, and doing so is, to a certain degree, beneficial to both body and mind. However, there is always the danger of overdoing it and getting out of control. We must be constantly on guard against this.

Our practitioners need to be alert to such deviating phenomena in qigong practice. I have said on many occasions that it is best for those people who have a history of mental illness, who are mentally disturbed, or whose family members are prone to mental diseases, to avoid practicing qigong without the close guidance of a qigong master.

When a practitioner detects deviation in his or her mental state, do the following immediately:

One, stop practicing for a period of time.

Two, study and analyze your own unconscious mind.

Three, consult medical professionals and accept psychiatric therapy.

Four, stay clear of all misguidance or temptation that may lead you deeper into error.

Five, rid yourself of all unfounded beliefs in qigong. Give yourself timely adjustment and guidance. Correct what has happened and refrain from being trapped into various illusions that may arise.

In qigong practice, some practitioners tend to be frightened by illusions of evil spirits or ghosts, but exhilarated to see those of Quan Yin Boddisattva or Buddha, believing it to be a sure sign of high level attainment. In truth, there is no Maya or Buddha in high level qigong attainment; none is necessary. Buddha is in your original mind, in your enlightenment and wisdom.

Eliminate Doubts and Anxieties

In qigong practice, many experience what I term unnecessary, ill-founded doubts and anxieties. Some of these people are normal and have a healthy mind before practice. Then they begin qigong and change entirely for the worse. They become so sensitive to so-called "ill qi" that wherever they go, the first thing they focus on is whether the qi there is good or bad. If they go to the hospital, they feel the "ill qi" everywhere. In the street, dirty qi is all around. If they happen to stand under a tree, they have to analyze the type of qi the tree may emit. When meeting others, they will decide this one has bad qi and should be avoided, while the other has good qi and may stay around more often. In all, they are filled with insecurity and anxiety. What then is the point of practicing qigong? They will be much better off if they do not practice so at least they can be normal human beings. Otherwise what they are doing is totally contrary to the purpose of qigong practice.

I know a woman who had a very nice personality and got along well with people. After she started practicing qigong she began to distrust people around her. Every time she went to a qigong event, she would feel someone sinister was trying to hurt her. Once home she would fall ill, with urinary bleeding or foot pain. She asked me whether she should go on with her practice.

I told her that first of all, it was her mind that caused all the trouble. In psychosis, there is a syndrome called "forced illusions," and one of the illusions is that the victim constantly feels someone wants to hurt him or her. In such cases, a person may have a normal personality but with a slight tendency toward forced illusion. Once the person practices qigong and experiences the relaxation of rational control, it is possible to induce the abnormal state described above. I told her that she must maintain an easy mind toward all things and trust in people, believing they are kind. If she could achieve these things, she would be able to continue practicing qigong. If she still felt out of control and continued to believe that others might harm her, then it would be better to stop practicing for some time.

Another man told me that after a period of qigong practice, he became afraid of going to public places to do his routines because he feared that other practitioners might steal his qi. He further elaborated on his point, saying that when practicing, a person's meridians are wide open and at such a time it would be easy for someone else to steal his qi or harm him, because in the group there was already someone who was evil. I laughed and told him to go ahead and steal qi from me if he could. He found he could not do it. Why? Because it is not easy to steal qi from a person.

I would not deny that it is possible to do harm using the force of qi, but it is a very rare occurrence. To the majority of practitioners, this should not be a source of anxiety. In China we have a saying, "Evil can never prevail over good." If your mind is at peace and aboveboard, no evil will ever prevail.

Unfounded anxiety can become a psychological hindrance in one's qigong practice. It may seem to be a simple problem, yet it is crucial to one's attainment of higher levels. Without eliminating this hindrance, we may as well play a lute before a cow than preach to these practitioners the importance of achieving higher levels.

Such anxiety not only affects your daily life, it also hinders your attaining the genuine state of qi. Qigong practice requires a peaceful mind without blockage, worry or desire. We must solve this problem before we can proceed further on our path of achievement. No matter how hard you force yourself, no peace of mind is possible, because your mind is not free nor at ease.

To some people, things were more normal before their practice. Now that they practice qigong, things are getting more complex and they become exhausted by overwhelming worries. Of course, for some this may pass and once they jump over the hurdle, their practice leaps to a higher level. However, if you let yourself be trapped at this stage, you will have a hard time progressing. In any qigong practice, instructors and masters must give correct guidance so practitioners are not trapped by superficial concepts.

In a deeper sense, these sorts of worries and anxieties are in reality part of Maya's control, the force of negative energy. Normally, those who are suspicious of others are more prone to interference from negative forces in their qigong practice, while more normal and stable people can easily avoid the influence of Maya.

Eliminate Restrictions and Taboos

Different people tend to have different concerns and restrictions. This is normal and nothing strange. By restrictions and taboos, I am talking about those unfounded inhibitions we sometimes encounter in qigong practice.

I know of a physician who was very devoted to her profession. She started practicing qigong because of health problems. She was introduced to the concept of "sick energy" and became extremely sensitive to it. Her work at the hospital began to cause her a lot of psychological inhibitions. After a period of time her health became worse than before. She was puzzled and frustrated. She told me she was able to see patients before she took up practicing qigong, in spite of ill health. Later every patient became a source of ill energy and she felt very exposed and vulnerable. She was afraid to go to work.

The purpose of practicing qigong is first and foremost to train our minds to reach the utmost peaceful state. Otherwise there is no use drilling ourselves in the different routines and movements. A doctor's duty is to help and heal, which should be a meritous deed. If qigong practice does not give more peace but instead causes more worries, it is better to stop practicing.

There are quite a number of practitioners who, once they acquire the so-called "qi" concept, avoid even a garbage truck in the distance, believing it contains malevolent energy. Before practicing, they had little or no restrictions. Now that they practice, everything becomes a restriction. What is this but a lack of enlightenment? While talking with many of these practitioners, I noticed that most of them are interested in obtaining some sort of archaic mantra or secret to boost their practice. What they neglect to see is that to reach high qigong levels one must break taboos.

Ill or negative energy certainly exists. The core of qigong is about qi, the energy that is in and around us. Does qi have any functional effects? No doubt. Otherwise, what is the purpose of practicing qigong? The rise of restrictions and taboos is a natural thing at the initial stages of practice. However, if we are trapped by various restrictions and taboos, we will not make progress.

Zen talks about enlightenment coming from a peaceful state of mind and the letting go of all worries, which also includes all restrictions. If we cannot let go of all these unhealthy and negative self-suggestions, it is difficult to continue practice and worse, it affects our normal day-to-day life, imposing strong psychological limitations. How do we expect to improve our practice?

When we encounter a certain psychological inhibition, we must first try to figure out its origin. Once we know the cause, then it is paramount that we free ourselves from its interference. Inhibition is another form of attachment. If we could detach ourselves from certain things, we would experience that enlightening moment and enter a higher state of being.

Since antiquity, mankind has suffered too many restrictions and inhibitions, whether in China or in other parts of the world. In our daily life, there must be millions of can-do's and can't-do's. If one was to believe every one of these restrictions, one would not be able to live a normal life, not to mention achieve high attainment of qigong. The best way is to be completely at ease with everything and anything.

In China we have a saying, "The killer who lays down his knife at once becomes a Buddha." Generally we would understand it as a moral teaching that advises wrongdoers to give up evil and achieve salvation. What we may overlook is the secret of qigong attainment embedded in this ancient saying. As soon as someone who has done something wrong realizes his wrong-doing and completely frees himself from its bondage, he immediately experiences the wisdom of life. No matter what kind of terror or frustration a practitioner has gone through, once he has set it aside he will almost certainly be able to experience the enlightenment of wisdom.

If we want to reach higher levels in our qigong practice, it is important to emphasize again and again that we must free our mind from all kinds of psychological burdens. Once that is done, we will naturally understand a great deal without deliberate effort and our practice will improve. We can detail all technical specifications of movements and routines, but we must know what higher levels are, and eventually reach that state of knowing without being conscious of knowing.

Prediction and Fortunetelling

The ability to know things before they happen is a form of psychic power. To a lot of people, it is both mysterious and fascinating. In China today, numerous books have been published on this subject. In my personal opinion, this archaic subject is worth our study and investigation.

Many methods of prediction used in the ancient times make a lot of sense. In the old times, there was no highly developed technology like we have today, but man was endowed with more acute intuitive powers than people today. Our ancestors evolved and expanded prediction methods from their intuitive understanding of heaven and earth, man and life.

In this oracular process, ancient men not only developed their methodologies but also experienced certain mysterious cycles of all things in the universe and in the universe itself. Many sages and wise men of the time studied and established a philosophy and moral system based on these studies. For example, Confucius's interpretation of the *I Ching, the Book of Changes,* and many of his other philosophical works came from such origins.

The secret of prophetic prediction is all in our God power. Human beings possess all knowing power in the subconscious mind. Whether one can make accurate predictions depends on whether one can call on the omniscient God power; that is, our subconscious.

In today's world, many ancient prophetic methods have been materialized as modern scientific forecast technology such as those used in weather forecasting or the measurement of cosmic bodies. Nevertheless, the study of ancient prophetic techniques is still relevant today because it can supplement modern scientific forecasting. It would be unnecessary to predict the movements of the solar system or forecast weather using ancient oracles. However, when it comes to the predictions of earthquakes or airplane accidents, modern science may still be in want of accurate predictions, and it is in such matters that oracles can play a part. As to the foretelling of our life events, it may be that ancient oracles are more significant in filling in the blanks.

In addition, the study of ancient oracular techniques may help us deepen our understanding of mind-body relations and the relationship of man and the universe which, in turn, will further the development of science and technology in our world today. I can see its prolific future ahead of us. I believe our study of the ancient oracular techniques affords a vantage point and unique perspective in unraveling the many secrets of man and the universe.

As related to our everyday life, we need to guard against being trapped in the superstitions of fortunetelling. Qigong practice should free us from all kinds of unnecessary worries and attachments. We want to be at ease with ourselves and others. What we need is enlightenment in all things, not warnings of things that may or may not happen. The truly Great Way should be the concern of mankind's future and our human civilization.

Formless is the Key

Elementary qigong practice usually starts with forms. These forms are routines that control the circulation of qi, enabling practitioners to open their meridians in order to be effective in strengthening the body and healing disease.

Form consists not only of body movements, but also the time and place of practice, moderate food in-take, state of mind and so forth. There are certain formatted postures, movements, and methodologies which we call forms. In the initial stage of practice, practitioners need to pay attention to details and specifics and acquire the standard movement routines. On the other hand, we should also be careful not to become too attached to the forms because it will also affect our improvement.

During practice, for example, the master says that for a certain routine the practitioner should face her palms up and lift her head slightly. The practitioner then tries to figure by exactly how many degrees she should keep her palms up or how much she should tilt her head. By focusing attention on such so-called specifics, she would not be able to experience the qi, and consequently cannot expect very good results in practice. As a rule, it is good enough to master the general routines without being too exact.

On the other hand, we should guard against another attachment; that is, the attachment to formless practice.

A qigong master may tell you that all forms are low level practice and he is teaching you the formless, the ultimate way of practice. In fact, his method will still be expressed through certain forms. There is no need to denigrate them, however, because they are expedient for the majority of people to practice. "Formless" refers more to a state of mind, of being. If you maintain a natural state of mind, regardless of what form you are practicing, it is formless.

There are others who are so fascinated by the formless way that they ignore the routine movements and neither pay attention nor train the mind. They think this is non-action when in reality it is not.

A friend of mine visited Beijing some time ago, and he wished to talk about qigong. I telephoned him one day. As soon as he picked up the phone, I asked him, "Are you sitting or standing right now?" He said, "I am sitting." So I said, "You have been asking me about the secret of qigong. Please adjust your sitting posture and make yourself more natural and more comfortable." He followed my instruction and told me he'd done that. I then asked, "Can you recall how you were sitting before I asked that you change your posture?" He thought for a long while and could remember nothing. I responded by saying, "There might be two possibilities. You rushed to pick up the phone when you heard it ringing, and sat down in quite an awkward position. It may also be possible that the position you sat in was the most natural, and no matter how you tried later on to adjust it, you would not be able to do the same." Similarly, when we deal with ten thousand people and things, the initial intuition, that flash of your original nature, is what we call "do without doing." It is something we need to experience. Just like the above example, the sitting posture can embody the very secret of qigong practice.

Ancient Zen masters had many methods of enlightening their disciples, and most of them were spontaneous, like the example I gave above. They used daily trivia to reveal some profound teaching. If we can return to and retain that natural state of the original self, we say we experience enlightenment. If we apply it in our qigong practice and our daily life, maintaining that state of mind, that is the genuine state of non-action. It is the higher level of qigong attainment, which may sound simple but is very difficult to achieve.

In qigong practice we often like to say that ten thousand ways will return to the Origin, and there is no fixed way to get to the Origin. The important thing is to go to the Origin; then no matter what way you are taking, you will achieve the ultimate level. Any qigong routine you follow will eventually lead you to the highest level.

There is no limit to practice. Experience at one level may be different from what we would experience at other levels. This is true for the majority of practitioners. At the highest level, however, there would be no differences—there would be no more high or low levels; everything and all things are the same. All forms are simply illusions. To attain this ultimate level we need to go slowly, one step at a time, just as one advances from elementary school to high school, then college, and finally earns a Ph.D. and becomes a professor, growing more and more learned in academic matters. The student may have to follow all the rules set by the grade school teachers; nonetheless the more he studies, the less he has to be bound by those rules. In spiritual practice the practitioner reaches complete freedom and ultimate liberation.

That is the state of original self, a state of nothingness. Someone asked me once, "What is our original self? What is enlightenment?" It would be difficult to define these concepts in words; we must experience it. Just like my favorite example of the taste of tea. No word can clearly define how tea tastes. Or to give another example, what is the color white? You may answer that it is the color of snow. But what is the color of snow? It is the color white. In a similar circle, we ask, what is enlightenment? It is our original self. What is our original self? It is our Buddha nature. What is our Buddha nature? It is our God power. What is our God power? It is enlightenment. We have returned to the beginning.

Returning to the Origin

Many practitioners wish to reach the secret of qigong practice. In reality, the secret is often the simplest, the most important. For example, some qigong masters heal patients by giving prescriptions. Sometimes the patient needs only to put the prescription on his or her body and will be cured without actually taking the medication. In some cases the qigong master only needs to use certain hand movements. In others, the master may need the assistance of certain posture or language. Some masters need the cooperation of the patient. There are all sorts of methods and all of them are just as effective in healing.

The secret is that all ways return to the origin, which is the

God power within us. If we can experience this, we will find it easy to understand the secrets of qigong.

Why is the prescription of a qigong master efficacious? An ordinary guy may write a hundred prescriptions and they will be useless. A person with healing power may use a prescription or transmission of qi or incantation, all of which are external forms. By using external help the qigong master maneuvers his qi, bringing his God power into play. What method the qigong master deploys depends on his or her own intuition. He or she will use whatever is most effective in calling up the healing power.

Of course, there are higher level qigong practitioners who do not need any external help, but can control their power at will. Methods are many and varied. We all go to the same place but each may take a different route. In qigong practice, the most important thing is to know and realize our God nature. It is such tremendous power. We all know it can perform miraculous healing. What if we can use it in our literary or scientific creations?

We all talk about enlightenment. It is a Zen term that means our mind is obscured. Then lights illumine and our mind is enlightened. That flash of the soul, that moment of illumination, is the origin to which all Ways return.

When we get to the origin, all secrets of qigong will become crystal clear, and we will enter the highest state of consciousness.

It is written in the *Tao Te Ching* that "heaven, by attaining the One becomes clear; Earth, by attaining the One becomes stable; Gods, by attaining the One become divine; Valleys, by attaining the One becomes full ... The Way gives birth to the One. What is the One? It is the Qi; it is the Beginning. Those who attain the One, attain the Tao, the ultimate Truth." Why is there "One-finger Zen" in Zen Buddhism? Let's all ponder this "One." When we reach a higher level of understanding, when we experience the "One," all is clear and there will be no more secrets.

Other Publications by
Abode of the Eternal Tao

Embarking On the Way: A Guide to Western Taoism
by Solala Towler
    Written in a simple and non-scholarly fashion, Embarking On the Way is designed to present the fascinating world of Taoist philosophy and practice to Western readers. It encompasses a wide range of Taoist studies, from the classical teachings of Lao Tzu and Chuang Tzu to the Tao of Sex and Relationship.
    Softcover, 160 pages, $14.95.

A Gathering of Cranes: Bringing the Tao to the West
by Solala Towler
    In this volume of interviews with nine well-known authors and teachers who have brought Taoism from China to the West, we learn the wisdom and experiences of Taoism, including meditation, qigong, taiji, and Chinese medicine, and receive guidance on how to live a healthy and long-lasting life—mentally, physically and spiritually.
    Softcover, 150 pages, $12.95

The Empty Vessel, A Journal of Contemporary Taoism
    A quarterly publication dedicated to the exploration and dissemination of nonreligious Taoist philosophy and practice. Learn practical applications of Taoist thought, tai ji, internal arts, Chinese medicine, and qigong. Enjoy articles, interviews and feature stories that show how contemporary practitioners have incorporated a balance of body, mind and spirit into their lives.
    Includes art, poetry, essays and reviews of the latest books, tapes and videos. The Empty Vessel is the only journal of its kind, covering all aspects of Taoist philosophy and practice in a thought-provoking and timely manner.
    Subscriptions are $18 per year. Sample issue $6.50 postpaid.

Abode of the Eternal Tao
1991 Garfield St. Eugene, OR 97405
Toll free order line: 1-800-574-5118.
See our website at http://www.abodetao.com/
for excerpts of these works.